Analysing Financial Perfor

Despite a plethora of techniques to analyse the financial performance of a business, there has been no single methodology that has been overwhelmingly preferred by users. This could be an indication that either the methods themselves are deficient or they are limited by other factors that are not easily overcome.

Unlike the current offerings in the field, which focus on issues relating to business performance management or non-financial aspects (such as market efficiency, satisfaction and workforce productivity), this book offers a solution to a major gap in the literature and understanding for those seeking to measure, analyse and benchmark the financial performance of any organisation (for-profit, not-for-profit and government agencies). It clearly identifies why current techniques fail; proposes and evidences a solution that overcomes these issues by including two algorithms that can be combined, to solve this problem; and demonstrates the practical application of the technique to the benefit of users in order to pinpoint real performance levels and insights. One of the largest issues this book will help to overcome is the inability to compare the accounts of businesses/organisations from different countries that report in different currencies. This technique eliminates the need for currency translations and the issues that arise with that process.

This book is an invaluable and practical guide to assist accounting and finance practitioners in measuring and comparing financial performance across firms with different business models, different accounting policies and different scales of operations.

Nic La Rosa, PhD (La Trobe University), CA, CPA is able to draw on over 30 years of industry experience managing complex organisational budgets and leading strategic planning, performance analysis and change management. Commencing his career with KPMG, Nic moved into a career of various executive financial and management roles across the tertiary, private and not-for-profit sectors. This includes roles as Chief Financial Officer (CFO), Manager Financial Performance Analysis, Business Analyst, Financial Accounting and Manager of Finance and Resources. With a PhD in economics and full accreditation and membership with Chartered Accountants of Australia and New Zealand (CAANZ) and CPA Australia, he has presented on his research at conferences and symposiums in Australia and the United States.

'The aim of the book is to provide the reader with an *innovative* approach to the use of standard accounting principles as a means of evaluating company performance. This aim is achieved via the debunking of several commonly held conventions in the accounting profession that are shown therein to be fallacious. To this end, this book may very well prove to be quite an *important* contribution to this stream of accounting and finance literature. Furthermore, I can safely suggest that it is of current interest to a potentially wide readership. It is also of potential long-term interest to anyone who (in, let's say, 20 years' time) will retrospectively study how the role of major 21st century crises (think GFC and COVID-19) *truly* affected firm value, in comparison to how the current/existing accounting "orthodoxy" would suggest. Thus, there is considerable potential for it to be relevant beyond the normal shelf-life of typical accounting and finance-themed books. To this end, one of the most attractive features of this book is its timing. Following the current economic shock, the environment will naturally be more open to new paradigms, and the accounting field is certainly no exception to this generality. In closing, I give this submission my highest possible endorsement.'

— *Dr Liam Lenten*, Adjunct Senior Lecturer,
Department of Economics, Finance and
Marketing, La Trobe University

Analysing Financial Performance

Using Integrated Ratio Analysis

Nic La Rosa

Routledge
Taylor & Francis Group

LONDON AND NEW YORK

First published 2021
by Routledge
2 Park Square, Milton Park, Abingdon, Oxon OX14 4RN

and by Routledge
52 Vanderbilt Avenue, New York, NY 10017

Routledge is an imprint of the Taylor & Francis Group, an informa business

British Library Cataloguing-in-Publication Data
A catalogue record for this book is available from the British Library

Library of Congress Cataloging-in-Publication Data
Names: La Rosa, Nic, author.
Title: Analysing financial performance: using integrated ratio
analysis / Nic La Rosa.
Description: Milton Park, Abingdon, Oxon; New York, NY:
Routledge, 2021. | Includes bibliographical references and index. |
Contents: Issues with currency and related financial performance
measurement techniques — Issues with percentages, ratios and
other attempts at absolute measurement scales — The proportional
asset ratio (PAR) as a solution — The anchored ratio (AR) —
Integrated ratio analysis.
Identifiers: LCCN 2020035379 (print) | LCCN 2020035380 (ebook) |
ISBN 9780367552527 (paperback) | ISBN 9780367552466 (hardback) |
ISBN 9781003092575 (ebook)
Subjects: LCSH: Ratio analysis. | Business enterprises—Finance.
Classification: LCC HF5681.R25 L33 2021 (print) |
LCC HF5681.R25 (ebook) | DDC 658.15/1—dc23
LC record available at https://lccn.loc.gov/2020035379
LC ebook record available at https://lccn.loc.gov/2020035380

ISBN: 978-0-367-55246-6 (hbk)
ISBN: 978-0-367-55252-7 (pbk)
ISBN: 978-1-003-09257-5 (ebk)

Typeset in Times New Roman
by codeMantra

This book is dedicated to my family for their love and support and sacrifices to allow me to do what I do.

Contents

Figures

Tables

Acknowledgements

I would like to acknowledge and thank the anonymous reviewers for their constructive feedback during the proposal process. It is a task that is necessary but otherwise unappreciated. I would like to thank Ms Kristina Abbotts (Senior Editor, Routledge) and Ms Christiana Mandizha (Editorial Assistant, Routledge), for their assistance, support and encouragement throughout the publication process.

1 Background and overview

Abstract

The aim of this chapter was to identify and explain the major reasons why currently utilised financial performance measurement systems fail to adequately fulfil their purpose. The four major problems that were identified were a lack of inherent context, the shortcomings of currency, perspective scale and temporal consistency. This chapter also explained how these issues negatively affected business financial performance measurement (BFPM) and analysis, and demonstrated that, because of these issues, current BFPM techniques are inadequate for their purpose.

Introduction

The practice of reporting, measuring and assessing the financial performance of organisations is a vital task for ensuring their financial well-being and longevity. Unfortunately, there are a number of issues that, to date, currently popular methods don't address, which is why those techniques do not adequately fulfil this objective. Although it is commonly understood that current techniques are flawed and inadequate for their stated purpose, there has been a lack of clarity about what the causes of this failure are. Without an understanding of what a potential solution needs to overcome, it would be difficult to truly appreciate the benefits of the methodology espoused in this book. The aim of this chapter, therefore, is to provide a brief background to the problem; to clearly identify and explain the issues to be overcome; and to introduce the system that overcomes these issues and will enable the fulfilment of the task of financial performance measurement and assessment.

Overview

Organisations may operate with different currencies, accounting policies, time periods and scales of operation. The analysis of the financial performance of those organisations would require the use of instruments that will enable valid direct comparisons between every organisation (and also in relation to the same organisation) over time. Such an instrument would increase the level of confidence in any conclusions that are derived from the data generated. The integrated ratio analysis methodology (IRAM) was originally created to satisfy the requirement for a robust instrument to assist with the comparative financial analysis of organisations. The range of applications for which the system can be utilised has, subsequently, expanded such that it possesses an enhanced utility for internal financial performance assessment requirements.

The IRAM overcomes a number of specific issues of concern relating to previous efforts to enable the assessment of the financial performance of organisations. This includes the effects of the time period selected for assessment, perspective scale and, more importantly, the shortcomings of the currency unit of measurement itself. This chapter provides a general overview of the history, developments and limitations that relate to the field of business financial performance measurement (BFPM). It will clarify the arguments that underpin the creation and development of the IRAM and demonstrate how this system overcomes the deficiencies of predecessors. The liberal use of examples and case studies throughout this book should not only ensure a thorough understanding of why it works, but also how the methodology should be applied in practice.

Although some of the potential benefits that could be enjoyed by practitioners and academics will be identified, it is likely that many more applications and benefits will be discovered by adopters of the system as the use of the methodology becomes more widespread and accepted. One example of potential benefits is the possible use of the IRAM in establishing universal standards of materiality for auditors. Another benefit from this system includes the improvement of homogeneity of data between different (and within specific) organisations. This will ensure that practitioners will benefit from more meaningful, consistent and accurate insights into the financial performance of organisations as stand-alone enterprises or when benchmarked to other enterprises. The benefits of this system could revolutionise the financial reporting practices of organisations globally as the expected utilisation from analysts should exponentially increase with the growing awareness of the advantages of the system.

This chapter will identify and illustrate why current financial performance techniques fail to enable qualitative assessments of the financial performance of organisations. This will be followed by an analysis of how traditional approaches that were adopted to report and measure financial performance (such as ratios and percentages) have failed to overcome these deficiencies. Understanding the flaws of these techniques and approaches will allow a greater appreciation for the abilities of the solution offered in this book to better meet the needs of the users of financial information. This solution is the application of one algorithm in two different time settings that, when applied in tandem, become a very powerful system to generate insights into the actual financial performance of any organisation. Once this system has been explained and demonstrated, this book utilises case studies and examples to help you understand how to apply the system for your own needs.

One application of the algorithm (the anchored ratio [AR]) converts the currency value of any variable into ratio values that absolutely *mirror* the patterns of the currency values over time. The ratio values, however, are a normalised version of the currency values and, therefore, enable the ratios for any organisation to be directly comparable to any other organisation irrespective of perspective scale. The other application of the algorithm (the proportional asset ratio [PAR]) provides a true level of significance (or performance) of every variable for a single period of time. This is independent of any results from prior or later periods of time. The simultaneous combination (or integration) of the AR and PAR techniques defines integrated ratio analysis. By overlaying the results of the two applications, an analyst can obtain instant clarity as to whether changes in the growth of financial variables are holistic (real) or not. No matter the purpose for the system to be utilised, the knowledge that it overcomes the identified shortcomings of other measurement systems should provide the confidence to employ it for financial performance measurement and analysis purposes.

Background

Measuring the financial performance of an organisation should be a simple exercise. This task involves money, which is measured in numbers, and so it could be expected that the greater the amount of money that is generated, then the better the financial performance would seem to be. The issue with financial performance measurement is not, however, the ability to *quantify* the financial performance of a business. The major difficulty that has been plaguing analysts is the inability to adequately assess the *quality* of a performance. Behn (2003, p. 586) succinctly summarised this notion by postulating 'Why measure performance? Because measuring performance is good. But how do we *know* it is good?' There are simply no accepted norms for what would constitute a *good* financial performance and even less agreement as to how 'good' such a performance would be.

In 2008, a company called ABC Learning that was listed on the Australian Securities Exchange (ASX) collapsed. It appeared that nobody was able to foresee this occurrence. For at least the five years prior to failure, all of the traditional financial performance metrics had been indicating that the business was performing exceptionally well. Indeed, the 2007 Annual Report touted a 115 per cent increase in revenue to AU$ 1.7 billion and a 76 per cent increase in profit after tax to AU$ 143.1million (ABC Learning Annual Report 2007). The share price during this period had increased from around the AU$ 2 mark in 2001 to just over AU$ 8 in 2006 (Rush and Downie, 2006, p. 217).

It appears that, while the market had no problem with quantifying the financial performance of ABC Learning, it didn't correctly appreciate the *quality* of that performance. Despite professional investors viewing ABC Learning as a very successful business, there was something fundamentally amiss about the actual performance that was not immediately apparent from the performance measurement systems available. If this was the case (and the evidence suggests that it was), then this was a failure that could have been prevented or, at the very least, the impact could have been minimised if the instruments used to measure the financial performance of the company were not fundamentally flawed. The pressure on managers and investors to make the correct resource allocation decisions is escalating as rapidly as technology and systems advancements are increasing. The need for methodologies that can reliably and accurately assist these decisions is, consequently, of paramount importance to such decision-makers.

This book will not only clearly explain and demonstrate what these flaws are, but also introduce a new measurement system that could have been used by the managers and investors of ABC Learning to avoid the failure altogether. The system in this book has been designed to provide a remedy for many of the deficiencies of current offerings in this field. It is believed that by eliminating many of the issues that reduce the reliability and comparability of traditional measures, this system will go a long way towards being able to answer the question of how 'good' a performance really was.

The need for business performance measurement

Much of the debate in this field has been centred upon the *purpose* of performance measurement. Behn (2003, p. 586) recognised this with the question, what '...is behind all of this measuring of performance? After all, neither the act of measuring performance nor the resulting data accomplishes anything itself...' Pike and Roos (2007, p. 218) further expand on this notion with the statement that, 'Performance measurement *assumes* that the results it provides and the benchmarking activities that accompany it are *useful in themselves*'. If the techniques and outcomes being performed and produced by the financial community are not the final objective, then it logically must follow that they are being employed to satisfy some other particular need or purpose. Indeed, Behn (2003) argues that performance measurement is being conducted in order to assist managers in achieving a number of specific managerial functions and purposes for which performance measures could prove to be useful. Behn (2003, p. 586) lists these purposes as '...to evaluate, control, budget, motivate, promote, celebrate, learn and improve'.

There is little need to elaborate upon Behn's efforts in this regard, given that the eight identified purposes could not only be neatly summarised into a mere three classifications, but further recognise that these three groups represent a cycle that continuously flows from one category to the other. The three categories in question are *planning* (budget), *control* (control, motivate, promote, celebrate and improve) and *assessment* (evaluate and learn). As one of the more cited authors in the field, Neely (1999, p. 205) aptly stated that, '...managers must have been planning and controlling the deployment of resources since the first organisation was established'. It could reasonably be expected, therefore, that this task would be aided by systems that provide management with insightful support for their strategic decisions relating to the maximisation of their allocation of resources.

Information to assist the decision-making process of managers is an important driver for business performance measurement systems. Once decisions have been made, however, measurement systems are required that enable managers, investors or other impartial analysts to assess the adequacy of that custodianship. As a consequence, the level of demand for techniques that can satisfy the requirement to adequately measure the quantity and quality of the financial performance of organisations cannot be underestimated. With both internal and external stakeholders of an organisation requiring a reliable method of measuring the financial performance of that business, it could reasonably be expected that such a technique would have already existed. Unfortunately, there are legitimate shortcomings that plague the existing measurement methodologies that have ensured that a uniformly supported instrument appears to be currently non-existent. In fact, Neely (2007, p. 3) presented a series of voluminous statistics of works and offerings in this field that only seem to support this notion. Only the absence of a clear and focussed solution would spawn such a fervour and diversity in the proposed solutions to satisfy these needs.

The economic dealings of a business with external parties have long been recorded and reported in financial statements. These financial statements, prepared utilising generally accepted principles of accounting, have long been the main conduit for assisting users of those documents to assess the financial performance and well-being of any organisational unit. If these documents successfully achieved this objective, there would be no need for any other measure of performance. The reality, however, is that the inability of this traditional means of reporting financial performance is so severe that '...over the past two decades a great deal of attention has been paid to the development and use of non-financial measures of performance...' (Otley, 2007, p. 11). A notable example of an effort to develop non-financial measures of performance is the balanced scorecard methodology proposed by Kaplan and Norton (1992).

The increasing interest in non-financial measures of organisational performance may be attributed to user dissatisfaction with the ability of financial statements to satisfy their needs in this regard. Indeed, Meyer (2007, p. 116) stated that '...the dissatisfaction that people experience with current measures and their yearning for better measures can be traced to an underlying but unrecognised cause. Superficially, the problem is measurement, and the solution is better measures'. While Neely (1999) identified shortcomings with financial statements in terms of how adequately (or, rather, inadequately) they addressed the needs of users, there is an overall absence in the literature of efforts to address the actual 'problem of measurement' when attempting to quantify the magnitude of the financial performance of an organisation.

In instances where attempts to stipulate shortcomings have been made (Neely, 1999, for example), they have tended to focus on issues relating to the level of usefulness of measures or quality of the underlying data, rather than an examination of the quality of the measure itself. The worth of any proposed alternatives cannot be reliably determined unless the reasons why traditional financial measures have fallen short of expectations are clearly identified. There may not need to be a concern about this, however, as arguments concerning the utility of performance measurement systems could, ultimately, be an entirely futile exercise. In the light of their philosophical nature, arguments relating to the uses of a performance measurement system would be almost impossible to resolve in a definitive manner.

This is because the usefulness of any instrument can only be validly assessed by the user of the mechanism, in the context of the use for which that instrument was employed. As such, it is felt that it would be far more productive if efforts were focussed on attempting to develop an instrument that has all of the characteristics of a quality measurement device, rather than on the uses for which such a tool could be employed. In this vacuum, it is the objective of this book to offer a system that will measure the financial performance of businesses that (as much as possible) will be free of the issues that create deficiencies for current financial measurement techniques and methodologies. This necessitates a process whereby the characteristics of an adequate instrument are identified; the shortcomings of existing methodologies are examined; and the proposed methodology is constructed, scrutinised and demonstrated.

What is 'business financial performance measurement'?

Lebas and Euske (2007) identified at least nine different possible meanings applicable to the word 'performance'. This ambiguity underscores the lack of consensus that was emphasised by Dumond (1994) and Franco-Santos et al. (2007) in terms of the literature's inability to define what is meant by the term 'business performance measurement' (BPM). There are, undeniably, many different aspects of the performance of an organisation that can be measured and reported. As such, there has been a significant growth in the literature concerning the development of non-financial measures of organisational performance (Kaplan and Norton, 1992, for example). Despite the purported superiority and notable levels of attention garnered by proposed substitutes (such as balanced scorecard reporting), it appears that these non-financial measures have not been unanimously supported, or adopted, by the business community.

Indeed, the American Accounting Association's Financial Accounting Standards Committee (The Committee) provided a noteworthy example of cautionary observations in relation to non-financial business performance measures in a 2002 report prepared for the Financial Accounting Standards Board (FASB). In deriving their conclusions, The Committee (2002, p. 2) determined that '...nonfinancial performance measures should be judged against the same criteria as financial performance measures, namely, the characteristics of relevance, reliability, and comparability espoused in the Australian Statement of Financial Accounting Standards No. 2, *Qualitative Characteristics of Accounting Information*'. Consequently, although their findings indicated that non-financial measures are valuable, useful and fundamentally reliable, The Committee concluded that in order for such measures to be relevant, they needed to be individually tailored to each business. For example, the non-financial key performance indicators (KPIs) for a service business would most likely be vastly different to those for a manufacturing business.

Unfortunately, the extent of specificity required for the adoption of non-financial measures will inevitably result in a significant diminution in the comparability of information from an inability to ensure the standardisation of measures. This issue was specifically referred to by The Committee (2002, p. 2), when they noted that '...users are hampered in their ability to use nonfinancial information by diversity in the types of measures and formats for reporting such measures' and that '...such an approach may limit direct comparability across companies...'. In fact, The Committee (2002, p. 8) summarised their views in relation to the impact of this issue with the statement that

> ...research suggests that investors' ability to use nonfinancial (and financial) information consistently across companies and time is impaired by noncomparability in measures or formats. Such noncomparability likely reduces the value of nonfinancial performance measures and may lead investors to focus primarily on financial measures for assessing performance.

An apparent preference by users to favour financial measures over non-financial measures is not at all surprising. In addition to the possibility of releasing proprietary information, it should be accepted that, no matter how intrinsically valuable to the *management* of the operational performance of a business non-financial efficiency and effectiveness measures may be, the majority of non-financial measures are ultimately correlated with the financial outcomes of the operations of a business. This understanding should not only promote the significance of financial measures above non-financial measures in terms of the comparability of measures, but this notion is further strengthened when it is combined with the observation by The Committee (2002, p. 1) that '...evidence indicates that managers tend to have difficulty specifying the relation between nonfinancial measures and future financial performance...'.

Indeed, there may be no need for a singular definitional panacea for this field if it is accepted that BPM is an all-encompassing phrase for any technique that is seeking to measure and quantify the performance of any aspect of the operations of a business. The definitional confusion generated by multiple aspects of business performance can be eliminated if any offering in this area simply modifies their use of the term to distinctly identify the aspect of business operations that is being specifically addressed. If, for instance, the object of interest relates to the analysis of the production function of a specific business, the BPM term could be modified to specify this particular focus such that it refers to 'business production efficiency measurement'. With this in mind, it should be noted that the IRAM has been purposely designed to address issues that are specific to BFPM.

Understanding that satisfying the needs of every potential user could be an impossible expectation to have of any methodology, this principle of commonality could assist the development of a financial performance measurement system that satisfies *most* users. As such, advocates and critics alike could be well served to remember the Pareto principle that it would be easier to satisfy 80 per cent of the population than the remaining 20 per cent and follow the path adopted by the accounting profession for financial statements. Acknowledging the Pareto approach to the preparation of financial statements (and the reliance of the IRAM on the data they contain), it could reasonably be expected that the IRAM will, at least, achieve a similarly high level of user satisfaction in relation to BFPM.

How is performance measured?

Regrettably, a combination of definitional discord, confusion of purpose and the legitimate shortcomings of existing methodologies has conspired in such a manner that a uniformly supported instrument is currently non-existent. It will be useful, therefore, to briefly examine general theoretical aspects of measurement and their specific application to financial matters at this time. Pike and Roos (2007, p. 218) describe 'measurement' as '...the process of assigning numbers to things in such a way that the relationships of the numbers reflect the relationships of the attributes being measured'. It is almost certain that any technique for measuring the financial performance of an organisation will fall into one of the five different types of measurement scales noted and described by Pike and Roos (2007, p. 231). These are (listed in ascending order of superiority) nominal (or categorical), ordinal, interval, ratio and absolute scales.

Nominal scales can only be used to identify that objects are different (e.g. male and female). It should be noted that because the only function of nominal scales is to classify subjects as possessing characteristics that are different to each other, they are not particularly useful for measuring and comparing performance on their own. As such, the methods and techniques that have been developed by the accounting community for the analysis of financial performance have tended to be based on one of the other forms of measurement scales. Ordinal scales extend this characteristic by additionally ranking the subjects in an order (e.g. from highest to lowest, or first to last). While accepted as being superior to, and containing the same characteristics of nominal and ordinal scales, interval scales lack a true zero point.

Although they enable calculations of the extent of a difference (e.g. 30°C as being 15°C higher than 15°C), the fact that the units of measurement are arbitrary means that judgements relating to their relative differences, such as 30°C being twice as large as 15°C, for example, cannot be made (Pike and Roos, 2007, p. 219). Although Gay and Diehl (1992, p. 153) identify that ratios scales are superior to interval scales because they possess a '...meaningful true *zero* point', they also recognise that absolute scales are the highest level of scale because all properties reflect the attribute in a one-to-one transformation. As such, an absolute scale-based solution would appear to be the ideal form of approach to satisfying the need to measure business performance.

The problems to be overcome

Regardless of the uses for which a performance measurement system can be employed, and disregarding whether such a system should have a focus that is historical or future based, every system that has ever been developed that purports to be for the purpose of measuring business performance is essentially seeking to answer the same question. Behn (2003, p. 586) succinctly summarised this notion by postulating 'Why measure performance? Because measuring performance is good. But how do we *know* it is good?' Although every user that inspects the financial statements of a business will be viewing the same reported performance, there is currently no mechanism that adequately enables a consensus opinion as to the *quality* of that performance. There are simply no accepted norms for what would constitute a *good* financial performance and even less agreement as to how 'good' such a performance would be.

Despite a plethora of proposed solutions, there is yet to be an instrument that effectively enables the measurement of business performance. Indeed, an international research workshop (conducted by KPMG's Assurance Research Institute; 2002) formally noted that there is yet to be a system that has been able to satisfactorily '...have a focus on long-term performance and still be relevant and capable of measuring performance in the short term'. Quite simply, there has been an historical absence of accepted norms for what would constitute a good financial performance and even less agreement as to how good such a performance would be. This deficiency in the qualitative assessment of the financial performance of an organisation is not limited to the trading result for any particular period of time. This shortcoming extends to every single value of any financial variable in any financial statement.

Numerous techniques and methods have been proposed and adopted over time that appear to help but, more often than not, actually exacerbate the problem. This is because there has been a lack of clarity around what the causes of this inadequacy are. The first issue of concern is that financial information is reported in units of currency. Unfortunately, currency is a demonstrably flawed unit of measurement and therefore an inadequate gauge of performance. The other issues that will be addressed include context, perspective scale, internal and external consistency, significance and temporal consistency.

In terms of assessing the financial performance of a business, the task is further compounded by issues of reliability and validity surrounding the measurement scales and instruments that have been available to date. The pressure on managers and investors to make the correct resource allocation decisions is escalating as rapidly as technology and systems advancements are increasing. The need for a methodology that can reliably and accurately assist these decisions is, consequently, of paramount importance to such decision-makers. The IRAM has been designed to be the tool that will provide the remedy for many of the deficiencies of current offerings in this field. It is believed that by eliminating many of the issues that reduce the reliability and comparability of traditional measures, the IRAM will go a long way towards being able to answer the question of how 'good' a performance really was.

Issues to be addressed

In noting that, 'Accounting measures of performance have been the traditional mainstay of quantitative approaches to organisational performance measurement', Otley (2007, p. 11) identified that historical perceptions of BFPM have been limited to the analytical interpretation of the financial statements of a business. It appears, however, that a rising discontent in the usefulness and reliability of the traditional financial methods utilised for this purpose has generated a prolific growth in interest in non-financial measures. Indeed, Otley (2007, p. 11) observed that '...over the past two decades a great deal of attention has been paid to the development and use of non-financial measures of performance...' (including such notable examples as balanced scorecards and performance prisms).

Accepting that they were promulgated in an attempt to satisfy the demand for a superior methodology, the merits of these proposed alternatives will not be examined herein. This is not to discount these alternatives in any way but, rather, it is considered that the financial performance of businesses is the characteristic that has the most relevance to the widest range of users. This will ensure that issues peculiar to those measures do not further complicate or confuse the matters specifically of interest for BFPM. It could be argued that the proliferation of literature expounding the virtues of these alternative measurement methodologies is sufficient evidence that traditional techniques are inadequate for their intended purpose. Neely (1999, p. 206), for example, reviewed the efforts of many authors that examined issues relating to traditional performance measures and summarised their criticisms by stating that '...they:

- Encourage short-termism...(Banks and Wheelwright, 1979; Hayes and Abernathy, 1980);
- Lack strategic focus and fail to provide data on quality, responsiveness and flexibility (Skinner, 1974);
- Encourage local optimisation, for example, "manufacturing" inventory to keep people and machines busy (Goldratt and Cox, 1986; Hall, 1983);
- Encourage managers to minimise the variances from standard rather than seek to improve continually (Schmenner, 1988; Turney and Anderson, 1989); and
- Fail to provide information on what customers want and how competitors are performing (Camp, 1989; Kaplan and Norton, 1992)'.

While accepting that these criticisms are entirely valid (and important), it is also noted that they are directed at the *utility* of existing measurement instruments. It appears that the focus has been on what is *done* with the measurements obtained and how well these systems satisfy the needs of the users of the information. What appears to be missing in the literature, however, is an assessment of whether the systems provide an acceptable *measure* of performance. There is an apparent failure in the literature to provide an objective method of determining what the adequacies and inadequacies of the traditional techniques they are intended to supersede may be.

In the light of the criticisms that were summarised by Neely (1999), it could be argued that the need for an alternative BFPM system has been encouraged by a general failure of financial statements to satisfy user requirements for the measurement of business performance. For this assertion to be supportable, there would need to be some element(s) or characteristic(s) that financial statements are lacking for them to be an inadequate means of conveying the financial performance of a business. The dearth of literature that has attempted such an analysis is not surprising. This is because any cursory examination of financial statements would be hard-pressed to identify any obvious deficiencies in their utilisation as a performance measurement system.

Utilising currency as a measurement unit, the financial statements of a business will present their financial information in a numerical format. Constructed to determine and report the trading result for a specific period of time, these reports appear to make it very simple to ascertain whether or not a business has performed positively during the specified time frame. Indeed, since the traditional presentation would include the prior period's results, even the magnitude of any change in performance can be ascertained by directly comparing the performances of the two reported periods.

In addition, given that the measurement unit of currency is consistently utilised among all businesses, even the modern inclination for 'benchmarking' to other businesses can be a relatively simple comparison of one business's financial statements to others. It can be argued that, despite the apparently positive features that financial statements are stated to possess, they are insufficient to satisfy the needs of the business community, as they presently exist (Neely, 1999). The overall aim of financial performance measurement is to provide users of financial information with an insight into the *quality* of a performance. This allows decisions to be made in allocating and managing the resources at the disposal of business managers, investors and creditors.

According to the traditional financial performance measures reported for ABC Learning, the company was performing extraordinarily well. As a result of this, its subsequent failure was completely unexpected. This situation will continue to occur for other organisations until the issues that currently render popular methods of financial performance measurement inadequate are completely understood. Ignoring philosophical arguments surrounding how financial statements fail to adequately convey the quality of business performance, it will be shown that there are four critical issues that render them (and other associated analytical techniques and methodologies) inadequate to satisfy the performance measurement needs of users.

The first issue is that, although reported in numerical values, the financial information contained in financial statements is devoid of an ability to instantly convey the significance of the values being reported. This characteristic is called inherent context. The second problem is that currency does not have many of the universal characteristics of a quality measurement unit. It does not, for instance, translate at a constant value between different currencies and nor does it inherently represent the same value over time. The third issue relates to the manner in which assessments of the financial performances of businesses may be influenced by differences in the relative or perspective scale of the operations of organisations under comparison.

While most current units of measurement can assist analysts to accurately determine *comparative* performances between businesses, they may be incapable of providing an adequate measure of *relative* performance if the scale of operations of the businesses under comparison significantly differ (perspective scale). The final issue to be addressed is that there is an identified inability for certain methods of analysis to provide a consistent, or accurate, measure of business performance for both short- and long-term time frames (temporal consistency).

Issue one: context

The financial implications of the activities conducted by businesses are recorded utilising accounting practices and summarised and reported in financial statements. As such, it is not surprising that the techniques and approaches adopted with the purpose of analysing the fiscal performance of businesses are generally reliant upon the information contained within those financial statements. The numerical nature of the currency associated

with the transactions that they report ensures that financial statements utilise money as their gauge for measurement. The seeming lack of ambiguity
surrounding numbers engenders a sense of confidence in our understanding of what they represent. Consequently, attempts to analyse the financial
performance of businesses will, inevitably, gravitate towards the use of
numbers to assist the judgement. Unfortunately, numbers have no inherent
significance other than 2 is larger than 1 by 1 (for example).

When utilised for *any* measurement task, numbers only acquire significance when they are *assigned* relevance via an exogenous reference point.
For instance, the performance of an athlete in a foot race is assessed by the
position that the athlete finished in the event. In this scenario, the number
1 is understood as being for first place and the number 2 signifies a second
place for the runner-up. In this example, the numbers 1 and 2 are *representative* of the final race positions. From a measurement perspective, when subjects are classified and ranked in the manner described for the foot race, it
is considered that an ordinal scale is being utilised. Unfortunately, as identified by Gay and Diehl (1992, p. 152), although '...ordinal scales do indicate
that some subjects are higher, or better, than others, they do not indicate
how much higher or better'. Consequently, other than signifying the outcome of the event, the example race positions will, regrettably, provide no
insight into the quality, or magnitude, of the performances.

For instance, while accepting that first place is the best possible position
in a race, would second place be considered a poor performance if that athlete had finished ahead of the previous world record time? Alternatively,
would first place be considered a good result if the athlete failed to finish
within a qualifying time for the final? In order for a measurement to be
meaningful, it not only requires a valid gauge, but also an appropriate context. Behn (2003, p. 598) further clarified this aspect by stating that

> Abstract measures are worthless. To use a performance measure – to
> extract information from it – a manager needs a specific, comparative
> gauge, plus an understanding of the relevant context. A truck has been
> driven 6 million. Six million what? ...miles ...feet ...inches?

In other words, a measurement must readily impart a clear understanding
of what has been measured.

The concept of a gauge and relevant context is critical for the purposes of
the measurement and quantification of the financial performance of organisations. This concept of context can be further refined to focus on the *inherent* context of a measure. If an analyst were presented with a measurement
value for *any* scale that they are intimately familiar with (such as weight,
height or length), they would immediately understand the significance of
the measurement. Measurements such as these would be reported with a
number and an associated non-numerical value that indicates what type of
measurement it was. The number represents the integer point on the scale

the measurement represents and the non-numerical value gives the 'context' of the value by expressing the gauge that has been used.

Any reported value for these examples will have *inherent* context because they do not require any additional information for someone to understand the magnitude and the significance of the measurement. Is 40°C hot? Is 300 km long? Is 0.0005 g heavy? Every one of these examples can be answered instantly without any additional information. This is possible because they possess *inherent* context. In 2008, ABC Learning made an after tax profit of AU$ 143.1 million. Can the question 'was that a *good* result?' be answered without *any* additional information? This result has all of the same ingredients of traditionally understood measurement scales. It has a number (143.1 million) and it has descriptors that indicate the gauge used (Australian dollar). Why then is this insufficient to reach a conclusion as to whether or not this was a good result?

The answer is that, when used as a measurement scale, currency does not possess the characteristic of inherent context. The absence of inherent context for financial information has resulted in the practice of presenting additional information in financial reports (such as prior period values). The provision of additional information in this manner is done so in order to assist users to establish an *external* context. That is, the additional information provides external points of comparison to imply some significance. Even within the same period of information, users compare the value for one variable (such as profit) to another variable for the same period (revenue, for example) in order to establish external (to the variable being assessed) context that may assist with assessing the quality of the financial performance of that variable. The absence of inherent context renders many traditional forms of financial performance measurement inadequate for the purpose they are being employed.

Issue two: shortcomings of currency

The complex and dynamic environment of modern trade and commerce is enabled by money, or monetary substitutes such as credit. Indeed, accounting practices ensure that all values reported for financial variables for a particular business in its financial statements are measured by the same unit value of currency. From this, it could be further surmised that if a number of different businesses report the particulars of their financial affairs in terms of the same currency unit, then this might engender a degree of confidence in the relativity of the variables between businesses. Unfortunately, however, the absolute nature of numbers can seduce an analyst of financial information into deriving conclusions that are not entirely accurate (or even misleading) because currency has certain limitations as a unit of measurement.

A key feature of a satisfactory measurement system is that the scale and measurement unit utilised not only enable measurements to occur, but also facilitate the communication of the measurements in a form that is easily interpretable and consistently comparable. For example, when numbers are used to convey a measure of distance, or weight, the reported values will always have consistent interpretation, no matter where in the world the measurements are taken and no matter in what time period. In addition, conversions from one unit of measurement will convert at a constant value to a different unit of measurement (imperial and metric units, for example). Unfortunately, due to issues with its inherent value and fluctuating conversion rates between different currencies, these are characteristics that currency does not naturally possess and, consequently, limit its worth as a unit of measurement for the purposes of BFPM.

Changing inherent value

Currency is a universally accepted medium of exchange that enables the transfer of wealth and goods and services. Divisibility and liquidity are characteristics that ensure that money is the superior option to enable this exchange to occur. These characteristics ensure that all units of wealth, or claims against wealth, are *measured* in terms of currency. This is also why currency has its own worth that is measured in the amount of goods and services it enables a consumer to purchase.

Described in numerical units of value, it is easy to believe that one currency unit today is precisely equivalent to the same currency unit 20 years ago. While this would hold true if the prices of goods and services remained constant, in reality, prices are continually changing (generally increasing) and, therefore, the price paid for an item in one period could be considerably different from the price paid for the same, or a similar item, in other periods. This means that, in periods of changing prices, the purchasing power of money and, therefore, its intrinsic value will be fluctuating. The amount of currency required for it to remain at the purchasing power equivalent of its historical value during periods of rising prices is directly inverse to the change in purchasing power.

For any measurement scale to maintain reliability and consistency, it should remain invariant to price changes over time and, therefore, any changes in the purchasing power of currency would diminish the effectiveness of currency as a unit of measurement. Fluctuations in purchasing power will not only reduce the additivity of the information contained within financial statements, but will also diminish its comparability. These characteristics not only render currency an imperfect unit of measurement, but also raise the question of whether of there is another scale that can be utilised to better facilitate direct comparison.

In order to maximise the characteristic of reliability, one of the key tenets of measurement is that the scale of measurement should remain invariant. Unfortunately, the inability of currency to maintain a uniform inherent worth over time in periods of inflation has significant implications for any analytical methodology that relies on currency values as the basis of its measurement scale. Regrettably, any changes in the purchasing power of currency over time will result in a significant reduction in the reliability of the values it represents and effectively renders currency as an imperfect unit of measurement. This is because fluctuations in purchasing power not only destroy the additivity of the information contained within financial statements, but also result in a reduction in the comparability of such information.

Issues relating to conversion

Another deficiency of currency is that it also lacks the characteristic of a consistent conversion rate. Although currency has numerical descriptors, it does not have the same characteristics associated with familiar units of measurement such as distance or weight. For these forms of measurement, conversions from one unit of measurement to a different unit of measurement will occur at a constant ratio. Examples include the conversion between imperial and metric units such as miles to kilometres and pounds to kilograms. The same cannot be said for conversion rates between different currencies. While it is known that allowances can be made for differences in the value of different currencies, the conversion rate from one unit of currency to another is, regrettably, rarely constant.

To illustrate the issue of conversion instability, the comparative exchange rates between three different currencies were obtained at two different points in time and summarised in Table 1.1 (as at 30 June 2010) and Table 1.2 (as at 30 June 2011). The volatility and unreliability of currency as a measurement unit is clearly evident from the magnitude of the percentage changes of the exchange rate values for the currencies being reviewed (refer to Table 1.3). This is highlighted by the degree of change in the conversion of US currency

Table 1.1 Comparative exchange rates at 30 June 2010[a]

	USD	GBP	AUD
USD	1	0.67	1.17
GBP	1.51	1	1.76
AUD	0.85	0.57	1

a Obtained from x-rates.com on 12 August 2011.

Table 1.2 Comparative exchange rates at 30 June 2011[a]

	USD	GBP	AUD
USD	1	0.62	0.93
GBP	1.6	1	1.49
AUD	1.07	0.67	1

a Obtained from x-rates.com on 12 August 2011.

Table 1.3 Percentage change in exchange rates of Tables
1.1 to 1.2[a]

	USD	GBP	AUD
USD	–	−7.46%	−20.51%
GBP	5.96%	–	−15.34%
AUD	25.88%	17.54%	–

a The percentages were calculated by deducting the 2011 values
in Table 1.2 from those in Table 1.1 and dividing the difference by the base and converting the result to a percentage.

(USD) into Australian currency (AUD) in just one year (25.88 per cent in the
first column of Table 1.3). The large variations in the values between these
three currencies clearly demonstrate that a simple translation from one currency to another could have an enormous effect on the outcomes of any
benchmarking exercise of the financial performance of businesses reporting
their information in different currencies.

Issue three: the influence of perspective scale

In instances where the performance of businesses is compared solely on the
outcomes of a single variable (such as profit), the selection of the superior
outcome can appear to be a relatively simple exercise. For instance, there
can be no argument in terms of which business generated the largest result
if the financial variable of profit is compared between businesses solely on
the basis of their currency value. If, therefore, the size of a trading result is
the only financial performance measurement of significance, then a simple
ranking analysis would be more than sufficient. Indeed, if all of the other
variables of the businesses being reviewed were comparatively equal, then
the conclusion derived from such an assessment could remain unquestiona-
ble. In reality, however, examples where there is equality in the operational
size of businesses being compared would be uncommon.

The implications of a disparity in the scale of operations of different businesses for the analysis of their financial performance could be significant.
The assumption that underlies this anxiety is that the larger the actual size
of operations, the more likely it will be that the numerical values of their
variables would alter in direct proportion to the scale of operations. This
implies that an apparently large surplus for one business may actually be
relatively equal to that of a business that generated a smaller numerical
surplus – once size has been eliminated as a variable. If comparative size is
not considered, then any conclusions that are made solely on the basis of the
numerical values of the respective surpluses (in terms of which was a 'better'
result) could be incorrectly derived. This concept can be termed *perspective
scale*, and the effect that it can have on the perceptions of the financial performance of businesses is underrated.

This concept is premised on the possibility that a business operating on a scale of thousands can be performing at a comparatively identical level to a business that is operating on a scale of millions. It is likely that a business that is operating on a scale of millions would find it easier to generate numerically larger values in their financial variables to those that a business that is operating on a scale of thousands could generate – simply because it is so much larger. However, if the objective of the comparison in performance was to determine which business performed 'better' in more qualitative terms, then any conclusions made solely on the basis of the numerical values of the respective trading results could be incorrectly derived.

It may be, for instance, that the numerically smaller business could be performing at the same level (or even superior) than the larger business – once the discrepancy in the size of the operations has been eliminated as a consideration. It could be that a business that has generated a numerically superior value for a variable from a comparatively much larger scale of operations than a competitor has achieved, may have accomplished this feat less efficiently compared to the outcome the smaller competitor attained.

The extent of this influence can be best illustrated through a simple example. The data that will be utilised for this example will consist of 2010 values for the two key variables of Total Assets and Fee Income of three professional bodies (AUSPA, UKPA and USPA). The Total Assets variable will act as a proxy for the operating scale of the different organisations. The larger the numerical value of the Total Assets variable, the larger the organisation is assumed to be. The Fee Income variable was selected as a financial performance indicator that most analysts would be interested in. This information is summarised in Table 1.4 and depicted in Figure 1.1.

Ignoring, for the moment, the fact that the Fee Income values are in different currencies, there would be a natural inclination to conclude that these businesses performed identifiably differently. However, once the Fee Income values are examined in *direct* relation to their corresponding Total Assets values, a linear relationship between the variables is revealed (as depicted in Figure 1.1). It follows, therefore, that if Total Assets are taken to be a proxy of the relative sizes of the different bodies, then the linear nature

Table 1.4 Key 2010 Financial data for three professional bodies[a]

Variable	USPA	UKPA	AUSPA
	USD	GBP	AUD
	('000)	('000)	('000)
Fee Income	1,07,821	38,884	58,250
Total Assets	2,25,663	33,057	95,164

a Obtained from 2010 Annual Reports.

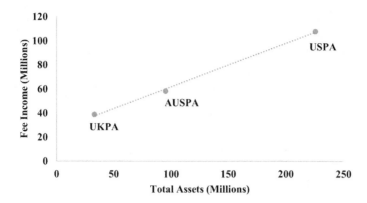

Figure 1.1 Direct comparison of Fee Income to Total Assets for three professional bodies[a].

a Obtained from 2010 Annual Reports.

of the relationship between these variables indicates that there may actually be *no* discernible difference between the *relative* performance of Fee Income for the three bodies when the *perspective scale* of operations is taken into account. This means that given the large disparity between the organisations in their Total Assets values, it would be questionable whether the numerical values of the trading results would be the best indicator of the quality of the results (performance) in this type of context.

This phenomenon is not confined to organisations reporting in different currencies. To illustrate this, the financial information for key variables from the published financial statements of four Australian banking organisations was selected. The banks that were selected for use in this illustration were the Commonwealth Bank of Australia (CBA), National Australia Bank (NAB), Westpac Banking Corporation (WBC) and The Bank of Queensland (BOQ). Total Assets and Total Income were the financial variables chosen for this example, and the data is summarised in Table 1.5 (for the financial year ending 30 June 2006).

After applying the same method to the information in Table 1.5 to that used for the professional bodies example, the resulting relationship depicted in Figure 1.2 indicates a linear relationship between the size of the Total Assets and the Total Income generated. This suggests that there may be no discernible difference between the *relative* performances of the banks selected for analysis (in terms of generating income) if the scale of operations could be normalised (were made to be equal). In both examples provided so far, the relationship between the income generated and their Total Assets has largely been linear. This supports the notion that a simple ranking of the numerical variables of variables is not an appropriate way to determine the quality of financial performance.

Table 1.5 Financial data of four Australian banks for financial year 30 June 2006[a]

Variable	CBA	NAB	WBC	BOQ
	AUD m	*AUD m*	*AUD m*	*AUD m*
Total Assets	3,69,103	4,84,785	2,99,578	15,797
Total Income	28,564	38,235	21,666	1,132

a Obtained from 2006 Annual Reports.

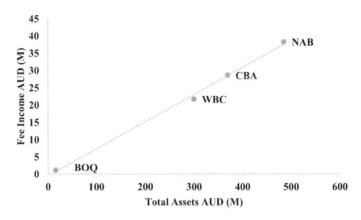

Figure 1.2 Direct comparison of Fee Income to Total Assets for four Australian banks[a].
a Obtained from Table 1.5.

Issue four: temporal consistency

As *time* is a method of categorical labelling for financial reporting, its use cannot, in itself, provide any form of utility. Despite this, the variable of time has a profound influence on the adequacy of some common financial performance assessment methodologies. It was shown, for example, that the use of currency as a measurement unit was flawed because its inherent value and conversion rates were not consistent over time. The issue of *temporal* consistency, however, considers the characteristic of consistency from a different point of view. Whereas the previously mentioned analysis of currency identified that the value that a measurement unit represented over time remained consistent over time, the concept of temporal consistency holds that the application of a technique should yield a consistent result regardless of whether it was applied in the short term or the long term. The review of the percentage change technique in the next chapter will illustrate this concept.

The solution

It could be thought of as inevitable that the failings of traditional financial measures would encourage the proposal of alternative methodologies. However, despite the existence of such offerings, it is felt that the non-financial nature of many of those examples is somewhat tangential and, therefore, an unnecessary distraction for the purposes of this book. While accepting that non-financial measures have their place, it is recognised that the primary responsibility of the accounting profession is to provide *financial* analytical expertise. Furthermore, regardless of the recognition that managers require information that assists them with business performance *management*, it is not intended to explore that aspect of business performance in any great detail. As such, the focus of this book will be confined to (and with a particular emphasis on) the *measurement* of the *financial* performance of organisations.

This objective can only be satiated through an appropriate instrument that enables the accurate measurement of the financial performance of a business. Accepting that there is a history of criticism levelled at traditional financial measures, it may be that accounting can, nevertheless, provide the foundation to ensure the fulfilment of this requirement. In fact, the techniques that are espoused herein – as part of the IRAM as a whole – form a solution that has been developed from the most elementary accounting rudiments. This ensures that the IRAM is free of some fundamental shortcomings of traditional methods. It also provides a measurement scale for financial performance that is free of major criticisms in relation to a series of characteristics that are essential to any scale that forms the basis of a measurement system.

In addition to complying with these essential characteristics, the IRAM enables analysts and management to concentrate upon critical areas of concern (or success) because this methodology is able to satisfy a characteristic of 'significance' that is often overlooked in relation to financial measurement systems. As identified by Neely (1999), this is a vitally useful attribute for those interested in the financial performance of organisations (in the light of the information overload they are often faced with). This is because it enables managers, analysts and other interested parties to filter out the noise and focus their concentration and efforts on variables that are *actually* significant.

Summary

The aim of this chapter was to identify and explain the major reasons why currently utilised financial performance measurement systems fail to adequately fulfil their purpose. The four major problems that were identified were (i) a lack of inherent context, (ii) the shortcomings of currency, (iii) perspective scale and (iv) temporal consistency. This chapter also explained how these issues negatively affected BFPM and analysis, and demonstrated that, because of these issues, current BFPM techniques are inadequate for their purpose.

References

ABC Learning, 2007. Annual Report 2007.

American Accounting Association's Financial Accounting Standards Committee, 2002. American Accounting Association's Financial Accounting Standards Committee Comments to the FASB on Nonfinancial Performance Measures. American Accounting Association, Financial Accounting Standards Committee. USA version.

AUSPA, 2010. CPA Australia Annual Report 2010.

Banks, R.I. and Wheelwright, S.C., 1979. Operations versus Strategy – Trading Tomorrow for Today. *Harvard Business Review*, May–June, pp. 112–120.

Behn, R.D., 2003. Why Measure Performance? Different Purposes Require Different Measures. *Public Administration Review*, 63(5), pp. 586–606.

BOQ, 2006. BOQ Bank of Queensland Annual Report 2006.

Camp, R.C., 1989. *Benchmarking – the Search for Industry Best Practices that Lead to Superior Performance.*Milwaukee, WI: ASQS Quality Press.

CBA, 2006. Commonwealth Bank of Australia Annual Report 2006.

Dumond, E.J., 1994. Making Best Use of Performance Measures and Information. *International Journal of Operations and Production Management*, 14(9), pp. 16–31.

Franco-Santos, M. et al., 2007. Towards a Definition of a Business Performance Measurement System. *International Journal of Operations and Production Management*, 27(8), pp. 784–801.

Gay, L., & Diehl, P., 1992. *Research Methods for Business and Management.* New York: Macmillan Publishing Company.

Goldratt, E.M. and Cox, J., 1986. *The Goal: Beating the Competition.* Hounslow: Creative Output Books.

Hall, R.W., 1983. *Zero Inventories.* Homewood, IL: Dow-Jones Irwin.

Hayes, R. and Abernathy, W., 1980. Managing Our Way to Economic Decline. *Harvard Business Review*, 61. pp. 67–77.

International Financial Reporting Standards (IFRS), 2011. The Official Standards and Interpretations Approved by the EU. Wiley and Sons.

Kaplan, R.S. and Norton, D.P., 1992. The Balanced Scorecard – Measures that Drive Performance. *Harvard Business Review*, 70(1), pp. 71–79.

KPMG's Assurance Research Institute. (2002). Summary Report: 1st Business Measurement Research Workshop. *The KPMG & UIUC Business Measurement Research Program* (p. 20). Illinois: KPMG's Assurance Research Institute. http://www.business.illinois.edu/kpmg-uiucresearch/roundtables/Copenhagen.pdf

Lebas, M. & Euske, K., 2007. A Conceptual and Operational Delineation of Performance. In: A. Neely, ed. *Business Performance Measurement: Unifying Theories and Integrating Practice.* Cambridge: Cambridge University Press, pp. 125–141.

Meyer, M., 2007. Finding Performance: The New Discipline in Management. In: A. Neely, ed. *Business Performance Measurement: Unifying Theories and Integrating Practice.* Cambridge: Cambridge University Press, pp. 113–124.

NAB, 2006. NAB National Australia Bank Annual Financial Report 2006.

Neely, A., 1999. The Performance Measurement Revolution: Why Now and What Next? *International Journal of Operations*, 19(2), pp. 205–228.

Neely, A., 2007. Introduction. In: A. Neely, ed. *Business Performance Measurement: Unifying Theories and Integrating Practice.* Cambridge: Cambridge University Press, pp. 1–7.

Otley, D., 2007. Accounting Performance Measurement: A Review of its Purposes and Practices. In: A. Neely, ed. *Business Performance Measurement: Unifying Theories and Integrating Practice.* Cambridge: Cambridge University Press, pp. 11–36.

Pike, S. and Roos, G., 2007. The Validity of Measurement Frameworks. In: A. Neely, ed. *Business Performance Measurement: Unifying Theories and Integrating Practices.* Cambridge: Cambridge University Press, pp. 218–237.

Rush, E. and Downie, C., 2006. ABC Learning Centres A Case Study of Australia's Largest Child Care Corporation. The Australia Institute, Discussion Paper 87. https://www.researchgate.net/publication/242275871_ABC_Learning_Centres_A_case_study_of_Australia's_largest_child_care_corporation

Schmenner, R.W., 1988. Escaping the Black Holes of Cost Accounting. *Business Horizons*, 31(1), January–February, pp. 66–72.

Skinner, W., 1974. The Decline, Fall and Renewal of Manufacturing. *Industrial Engineering*, October, pp. 32–38.

Turney, P.B.B. and Anderson, B., 1989. Accounting for Continuous Improvement. *Sloan Management Review*, 30(2), pp. 37–48.

UKPA, 2010. CIMA Chartered Institute of Management Accountants, Financial Statements 2010.

USPA, 2010. AICPA American Institute of CPAs, Annual Report 2010.

WBC, 2006. Westpac Annual Financial Report 2006.

2   Issues with currency and related financial performance measurement techniques

Abstract

The fundamental unit of measurement for financial reporting purposes is currency. All financial statements report the activities of a business using currency values. Unfortunately, currency is an inadequate unit of measurement as it is unable to overcome issues of inherent context, temporal consistency, inherent worth, consistent conversion and perspective scale. This chapter explored what these issues were and how, as a result of their influence, rendered currency an imperfect unit of measurement and any technique that relied on them to measure financial performance inadequate for purpose.

Introduction

The financial information contained in the financial statements (trading statement and balance sheet) of any organisation is all reported in currency values. Regrettably, there are a number of issues that limit the utility of this information. While there are criticisms from many quarters about the utility of the financial statements themselves, it is the efficacy of the measurement unit of currency itself that is the primary concern here. The predominant issues that result in currency being a flawed unit of measurement were identified in Chapter 1. In addition to the fact that currency has an inherent worth (which is unique for a measurement scale) that is variant over time, these issues include a lack of a consistent conversion rate and an absence of inherent context. Although these issues are widely known, it is important for the understanding of the promoted integrated ratio analysis to examine them so as to build the foundations of later analysis. This chapter will illustrate and expound upon the inadequacies of currency as a measurement unit and provide case study examples of its shortcomings.

Currency as a measurement scale

The financial dealings of the operations of an organisation are reported to management and external stakeholders through a set of financial statements.

The information contained in these documents is used for many different purposes depending upon the specific needs of the consumers of that information. No matter what the purpose is, however, the analysis of that information must rely upon the numerical currency values that those statements report as the measurement scale to be relied upon. The trading statement seeks to report the performance of the ability of an organisation to manage their operations so that they are generating more revenue than the resources they expend to generate that income. The activities summarised in such reports are for a specific period of time. This can range from periods as little as weekly to, more typically, yearly periods of time. The other major financial statement is the balance sheet. This document reports the total resources an organisation has at its disposal (as reported in currency values) and the claims against these resources from creditors (liabilities) and the owners (proprietorship). In contrast to the trading statements, the period of time that this document is prepared for is at one specific date in time. This difference between the two statements in the perspective of time frames can result in users treating the statements as being completely separate documents when they are actually inter-related.

An example of the key variable groupings from these financial statements is presented in Table 2.1. This table contains the financial information for a select number of key financial variable categories that were obtained from the 2010 financial statements of three international professional associations (AUSPA, UKPA and USPA). Despite being not-for-profit entities, these associations were deliberately selected because they essentially provide the same services and report their operations using different currencies. In addition to forming a base for later analysis, the immediate purpose of this information is to demonstrate the limited utility from the presentation of data for accounting variables in currency units. For instance, it may appear that, because the data represents the same financial variables, the same time period, and is reported numerically, it is simple to draw conclusions about the comparative financial performance of the organisations in this example. Unfortunately, there can be very little meaningful comparisons or insights made between these bodies because the information provided is based on

Table 2.1 Key financial data for international professional associations for 2010[a]

Variable	USPA	UKPA	AUSPA
	USD	GBP	AUD
	('000)	('000)	('000)
Fee Income	1,07,821	38,884	58,250
Surplus	8,856	1,089	11,807
Total Assets	2,25,663	33,057	95,164
Total Liabilities	1,77,312	20,867	46,844
Total Equity	48,351	12,190	48,320

a Obtained from 2010 Annual Reports.

different currency 'scales'. The sections that follow will not only address the issue of different currencies and problems with their conversion, but also address the other issues to do with currency as a measurement unit that were identified in Chapter 1.

Inherent context

One of the key strengths of a quality measurement scale is that they should possess the quality of inherent context. That is, there is no need for additional information to enable a user to understand the implications of the measurement being reported. Currency does not possess this quality to the same extent as the more commonly used measurement scales. Temporarily disregarding the fact that the information in Table 2.1 is reported in different currencies, the issue of inherent context already complicates the task of financial performance assessment. There is very little utility that can be ascertained from any single variable for any single organisation in Table 2.1 simply because the information presented lacks inherent context.

The 'Surplus' variable in a trading statement is the only 'calculated' variable in the accounting statements. While every other variable is a stand-alone value that represents specific items, the trading result (Surplus, for example) only arises once the expenses of an organisation are deducted from the revenue of the organisation. This means that, of all of the accounting variables that are reported in currency values, the 'Surplus' is the *only* one that has some naturally *inherent* context. When a trading result (surplus or deficit) is reported, all consumers of that information understand that this value is more (surplus) or less (deficit) than the revenue that organisation generated. The currency value of the trading result *quantifies* how much more or less than revenue has been expended.

A characteristic such as this could lead to the conclusion that this is the ultimate measure of financial performance for an organisation. After all, the assumed objective of free-market competitive firm is that it is profit-maximising. This should mean that the larger the size of the surplus, the better the financial performance of an entity has been. If currency truly possessed the characteristic of inherent context, then this conclusion would be fully supportable. Unfortunately, however, despite currency providing the ability to *quantify* the trading performance of an organisation, it is incapable, of its own accord, of providing an insight into the *quality* of a financial performance. A simple illustration of this point is the trading result for 2010 for USPA in Table 2.1. The Surplus for USPA in 2010 was $8.8 million (refer to Table 2.1). This result was positive and, from most points of view, a sizeable number. This has quantified the trading result for USPA for 2010. Other than acknowledging that the result was positive and a sizeable number, however, there is nothing in this single value that enables an analyst to determine *how* good this result was *for* USPA.

If currency possessed the same measurement characteristics as the measurement scales for weight, for example, the trading result would have true inherent context. A reported air temperature of 40°C (104°F) would instantly convey that the temperature was not only hot (quantify), but that it was *very* hot (qualify) for all users. Unfortunately, in order to generate some level of appreciation of the quality of the currency value Surplus for USPA, the reported value of $8.8 million must be compared to other variables such as the size of the Total Assets or Fee Income, for example, for some *external* (to the value being assessed) context to try and determine whether the Surplus was at a level to qualify it as a 'good' performance. Based solely on the reported currency values of financial variables, questions such as these cannot be properly (and instantly) answered because of the lack of inherent context for currency as a measurement unit.

Currency and rates of conversion

It is likely that, even if the Surplus for USPA was compared to other internal variables for context, it may still not be sufficient to answer the question of whether the result was a good one for that organisation. This is where analysts have found the practice of benchmarking to the results from external entities to be beneficial. This practice essentially seeks to answer the question of whether the values for the organisation of specific interest are better, or worse, than similar organisations. If currency was a measurement scale of sufficient quality, this task would consist of determining trends in the values of variables over time utilising some mental arithmetic. At the very minimum, a simple assessment of which values are the largest is involved. The technique of ordinal ranking is a way to formalise this process. The application of an ordinal ranking scale involves any procedure that requires the listing, ranking or ordering of a collection of data according to a predetermined rule. Examples of such rules include (but are not limited to) smallest-to-largest, heaviest-to-lightest and coldest-to-hottest.

Noting that the information is reported in different currencies, the surplus values of the three professional bodies listed in Table 2.1 were selected for this exercise. The rule that was applied for this example was highest-to-lowest, and this was based on an assumption that the larger the surplus amount, the better the outcome is adjudged to be. The application of this ordinal ranking rule to the surplus values listed in Table 2.1 results in the order presented in Table 2.2. If the values in Table 2.2 were reported in the same currency, the ranking outcome of these values would be totally valid

Table 2.2 Ordinal ranking of 2010 Surplus (in currency values) of Table 2.1 organisations from largest-to-smallest

Ordinal ranking	Organisation	Surplus
1	AUSPA	11,807,000 (AUD)
2	USPA	8,856,000 (USD)
3	UKPA	1,089,000 (GBP)

and there would be no need for further action. However, this result would be the equivalent of ranking three weight measurements that are reported in different measurement scales without being converted. It could be that once the currency values have been converted into a single currency unit, the order listed in Table 2.1 may actually change.

To reflect this reality, the information in Table 2.2 was converted into USD at the exchange rates at 30 June 2010 from Table 1.2. The converted values from this translation are reported in Table 2.3. The results listed in Table 2.3 have also been subjected to the application of the ordinal ranking rule of largest-to-smallest. Although the new values for this particular example did not result in any change to the ranking order of the three organisations in the example, the differences between the actual numbers reported have changed. The fact that they are now all reported on the *same* currency scale means that the ranking reported in Table 2.3 is a legitimate outcome of values that are reported on the same scale.

If the conversion rate between these currencies never altered in the same way that conversions for distance, weight and temperature would not, then this issue could rest here. However, if the rates of exchange from 30 June 2011 were utilised for this exercise instead (taken from Table 1.3), the converted values for Table 2.2 (refer to Table 2.4) would differ from the values reported in Table 2.3 and would, therefore, reflect the inconsistent outcomes from having translation values that can alter over time. Although the actual ranking of the results in this example did not alter at all for any of the reported (and translated) currency values, the numerical differences between

Table 2.3 Ordinal ranking of 2010 Surplus (in USD at 30/6/2010) of Table 2.1 organisations from largest-to-smallest[a]

Ordinal ranking	Organisation	Surplus
1	AUSPA	10,036,000 (USD)
2	USPA	8,856,000 (USD)
3	UKPA	1,644,000 (USD)

a Converted from their natural currencies in Table 2.1 into USD using the exchange rates from Table 1.1.

Table 2.4 Ordinal ranking of 2010 Surplus (in USD at 30/6/2011) of Table 2.1 organisations from largest-to-smallest[a]

Ordinal ranking	Organisation	Surplus
1	AUSPA	12,633,000 (USD)
2	USPA	8,856,000 (USD)
3	UKPA	1,742,000 (USD)

a Converted from their natural currencies in Table 2.1 into USD using the exchange rates from Table 1.2.

the different results in this example have changed dramatically. This could imply different levels of performance for the same results simply because of the date of translation selected for the conversion. This example illustrates that an inconstant conversion rate diminishes the utility of currency as a financial performance measurement scale. Furthermore, irrespective of this complication, the outputs of the ordinal ranking of financial information only allow an analyst to determine which variables had the highest values and not whether this actually equated to *better* performances.

Currency measurements and perspective scale

The ordinal ranking of values reported on traditionally understood measurement scales (such as weight, height and length) would convey any actual differences in the results – so long as they had been converted to the same scale. The reason that the results for currency values reported in the financial statements cannot provide the same utility as other measures (irrespective of translation to the same currency) is that the effects of perspective scale negatively impact the perception of currency values. A value that is related to a measurement scale such as weight or length is naturally independent. For this reason, whether a measurement on these scales is larger, or smaller, than another measurement, and by how much, can be independently assessed. This is not the case for the currency values of variables reported in financial statements. The value of any individual financial variable is actually dependent on other financial variables in terms of their relative quality.

As such, the currency values of financial statement variables cannot be directly compared between organisations – even if they are reported in the same currency. For example, although the air temperature of one city in a country can be critically compared to the air temperature of any other city without any other consideration, because of perspective scale, the same cannot be said for the currency value of one organisation in comparison to any other organisation. The results that have been ranked on an ordinal basis of largest-to-smallest in Table 2.3 can be used to illustrate this problem. Although, for example, the trading result for USPA in Table 2.3 is $7.212 million *bigger* than the $1.644 million result for UKPA, it does not automatically mean *better*. When assessing the financial performance of different organisations in a benchmarking exercise, it is important to consider the comparative sizes of those organisations.

The Total Assets values for the three example organisations in Table 2.1 indicate that, numerically, the size of the three organisations differs markedly. As was illustrated in Chapter 1, the size of a trading result for these organisations could be expected to proportionally increase with the Total Assets (proxy size) of the organisation and, therefore, an ordinal ranking of variable values that have not been adjusted to reflect this perspective would have little utility. Even though they have not been converted to a standard unit of currency, the Total Assets values for USPA and UKPA in Table 2.1 still demonstrate how perspective scale can influence the perceptions about financial performance. For instance, the trading result for USPA of $8.856 million in Table 2.3 was 5.4 times the size of the $1.644 million result for UKPA. This result may not appear as impressive when it is considered that the size of Total Assets for USPA of $225.663 million is 6.8 times the size of the Total Assets value of £33.057 million for UKPA (even though they have not been converted to a common currency).

Case study: currency value analysis for General Motors (GM)

In order to illustrate the various issues and demonstrate the different techniques that will be examined throughout this book, a business from the well-known US Fortune 500 list was selected for analysis. As such, and with the additional intention of forming a base for later analysis, the financial statement values reported in the Annual Reports for the 2009–2011 financial years of General Motors (GM) have been summarised in Figure 2.1. The values listed in Figure 2.1 reflect the USD currency values of the identified trading statement and balance sheet variables for the selected time periods.

Given that the information reported is of a numerical nature, it would be easy to believe that assessing the level of financial performance of GM over the time frame selected would be a relatively simple objective to satisfy. Unfortunately, there can be no such assessment made for any individual value for any individual variable (even for Operating Income/Loss) simply by the number it has been assigned. This lack of inherent context is one of the major drawbacks of currency as a measurement scale for the financial performance measurement of organisations. For example, the Automotive Sales for GM for 2009 was $104,589 million (refer to Figure 2.1). When examined individually, there is not a lot that can be interpreted about the performance of GM in relation to this variable for this period. The result was what it was. There is no instant and inherent reference to ascertain the quality of this value.

With a lack of inherent context for the currency value of the 2009 Automotive Sales variable, this can be compared to the level of revenue this segment of operations generated in the period prior and, or, the period following than the one being examined. The underlying aim of this form of assessment is to enable users to compare the values of financial variables to those of other periods. This practice is a process of *internal* benchmarking to find context that is 'external' to the value that is specifically being assessed. This technique allows an analyst to determine if the value for one period has been an improvement in terms of a direct comparison to another value. Such a conclusion would be based on the assumption that if the 2010 revenue was larger than the 2009 revenue, for example, then the result was better.

This purpose could be seen to encourage the practice of reporting the financial information of more than one period at a time (usually at least one preceding period). This form of presentation should enable users to ascertain whether the time-comparable values for the variables under analysis have moved and in what direction. The utility and validity of this practice, however, is severely limited by the impact of changes in perspective scale. If, for example, GM increased its operations by means of expansion, or new business activity, then numerical growth in revenue could be naturally

		2009	2010	2011
		USD m	USD m	USD m
Trading Statement				
Revenue				
Automotive Sales		104,589	135,142	148,866
GM Financial Revenue		0	281	1,410
	Total Revenue	104,589	135,423	150,276
Expenses				
Automotive Cost of Sales		112,130	118,768	130,386
GM Financial Expenses		0	152	785
Automotive Selling, General & Admin		12,167	11,446	12,105
Other Automotive Expenses		1,250	118	58
Goodwill Impairment		0	0	1,286
	Total Costs & Expenses	125,547	130,484	144,620
	Operating Income /(Loss)	-20,958	4,939	5,656
Balance Sheet				
Assets				
Automotive Current Assets		59,247	53,053	60,247
Automotive Non-Current Assets		77,048	74,913	71,313
GM Financial Assets		0	10,932	13,043
	Total Assets	136,295	138,898	144,603
Liabilities				
Automotive Current Liabilities		52,435	47,157	48,932
Automotive Non-Current Liabilities		54,905	47,223	47,860
GM Finance Liabilities		0	7,359	8,820
	Total Liabilities	107,340	101,739	105,612
	Net Assets	28,955	37,159	38,991
Equity		28,955	37,159	38,991
	Total Equity	28,955	37,159	38,991

Figure 2.1 Financial summary for GM 2009–2011[a].

a Obtained from the 2009 to 2011 financial statements for GM.

expected. Any review of a financial variable without this aspect being taken into account will not produce an accurate conclusion about the performance of that variable.

Using the internal comparative benchmarking process, it can be concluded that the Total Revenue for GM over the three-year period in Figure 2.1 has demonstrably consistently increased over that time. Understanding that income is a positive influence on the wealth of a business, this is clearly a favourable outcome. However, over the same period of time, the Total Expenses for GM has also consistently increased. Because expenditure is a negative influence on the wealth of a business, this trend would generally be considered an unfavourable outcome. Further analysis of the expenditure in Figure 2.1 reveals that the values reported for Other Automotive Expenses appear to have declined over the time frame examined. Again, as expenditure is a negative outflow of resources, this reduction indicates an improvement in the financial position of GM.

In terms of the overall operating financial performance for GM, the most encouraging aspect of the information in Figure 2.1 is that the Operating Income/Loss values reported over this time have been increasing. This is, in turn, reflected in the balance sheet where it could also be stated that a positive trend (increasing values over time) in the Net Assets reported in Figure 2.1 for GM indicates that the overall financial position of GM has improved in the time frame examined. Unfortunately, although analytical statements such as these can be made because there are comparative values for a number of periods, financial information prepared and presented using only currency values cannot specify which performance was *actually* better or worse.

Ordinal ranking assessment of GM financial variable currency values

The process for ordinal ranking, utilising the ordinal rule of smallest-to-largest, was applied to the Total Revenue for GM for the three financial years ending 2009–2011 (as reported in Figure 2.1). The results of this process are reported in Table 2.5. Noting that revenue is a positive influence on wealth creation, the fact that Total Revenue for GM has increased over the time frame examined would encourage an analyst to believe that GM has performed positively over that time frame. It may not be sufficient, however, to know that a result in one time period is larger, or smaller, than the value for the same variable from another time period. In itself, this knowledge does not necessarily indicate that one result is better than another one. It may simply be that such information only indicates the comparative difference between a variety of different results.

Expenditure is a negative influence on wealth, as it requires an outflow of resources to enable it to occur. As such, the Total Expenditure for GM for the financial years 2009–2011 of GM (as reported in Figure 2.1) was also ranked. However, this time the ordinal rule that was applied was the smallest value to

Table 2.5 Ordinal ranking of GM Revenue in financial years 2009–2011 from largest-to-smallest[a]

Ordinal ranking	Financial year	Total Revenue (USD million)
1	2011	1,50,276
2	2010	1,35,423
3	2009	1,04,589

a Obtained from the Figure 2.1.

Table 2.6 Ordinal ranking of GM expenditure in financial years 2009–2011 from smallest-to-largest[a]

Ordinal ranking	Financial year	Total Expenditure (USD million)
1	2009	1,25,547
2	2010	1,30,484
3	2011	1,44,620

a Obtained from the Figure 2.1.

the largest (on the assumption that smaller expenditure values are better than larger ones). The values for this variable (obtained from Figure 2.1) indicate that the performance for the expenditure in the individual periods examined has reversed in comparison to that which was reported for the application of the ordinal ranking rule to Total Revenue. That is, whereas the 2009 result for Total Income was the 'worst' result, it was the 'best' performing period in terms of the lowest level of reported Total Expenditure. Again, apart from ranking results according to their comparative sizes, this exercise cannot truly inform an analyst as to which period reported the 'best' value for Total Expenditure. In reality, Total Expenditure and Total Revenue are inextricably related. The performance of those variables must normally be considered in the context of each other to enable adequate consideration of whether either variable had performed 'well' or not. To this point, no technique examined so far has enabled an analyst to ascertain whether the result for any *individual* variable in any *individual* period was 'good' or not (Table 2.6).

It may be that, to obtain any benefit from the ordinal ranking system of financial information, users will need to focus on variables that could help them better interpret the results from other variables. To test this possibility, the trading result values for GM over the time frame examined and reported in Figure 2.1 were ranked using the ordinal ranking rule of largest-to-smallest. The Surplus variable was selected because it represents the net contribution to resources from trading (the net result of deducting Expenditure from Revenue). Ideally, this would result in positive values and contribute to the overall financial wealth of a business. The results of this process for GM are reported in Table 2.7. Given that an operating result represents the net outcome of the interaction between Revenue and Expenditure, it would be reasonable to assume that a larger result is automatically better than a smaller result. On this basis, the Surplus result for 2011 in Table 2.7 can be deemed to be 'better' than the result reported for the 2010 financial year by virtue of the value being larger. Although this is intuitively correct, we cannot know (based on these values alone) whether it was, in fact, a *better* result. Again, this is because the conclusion has been made in a vacuum of any context. How much Revenue was required to obtain those values? How large was the value of resources employed to generate those results?

In order to ascertain whether the level of resources may have had an impact on the financial performance of GM for 2009–2011, the ordinal ranking process was applied to the Total Assets values reported for those years. Utilising the ordinal ranking rule of largest-to-smallest to rank the Total Assets values for GM for the financial years ending 2009–2011 results in the outcomes reported in Table 2.8. Understanding that the Total Assets values for GM were steadily increasing over the time frame examined, it would be reasonable to expect that Revenue and Surpluses would also increase over that time frame. This assumption is based on evidence (refer to Chapter 1) that the numerical size of Revenue that an organisation is able to generate, is directly related to the size of its Total Assets. It is similarly assumed that the numerical size of surpluses would be associated with the numerical size of the Total Assets of a firm. Noting that the Revenue (refer to Table 2.5) and Surpluses (refer to Table 2.7) for GM did, in fact, increase over the time period being examined, this outcome casts further confusion as to just how well these variables performed during the period of analysis, when considered solely on their currency values.

Table 2.7 Ordinal ranking of GM Surplus in financial years 2009–2011 from largest-to-smallest[a]

Ordinal ranking	Financial year	Operating result (USD million)
1	2011	5,656
2	2010	4,939
3	2009	−20,958

a Obtained from the Figure 2.1.

Table 2.8 Ordinal ranking of GM Total Assets in financial years 2009–2011 from largest-to-smallest[a]

Ordinal ranking	Financial year	Total Assets (USD million)
1	2011	1,44,603
2	2010	1,38,898
3	2009	1,36,295

a Obtained from the Figure 2.1.

Assessment of currency as a financial performance measurement unit

While the inherent characteristics of currency may render it as an imperfect unit of measurement, financial statement values that rely on this measure will, nevertheless, provide the users of these statements with some level of utility. Despite this, an understanding of the limitations of the information in accounting statements can help users to assess the level of risk they face when considering any decisions relying solely on that information. The use of the ordinal ranking scale for financial information is a simple way to determine how the value of a particular variable compares to the value of the same variable from another time period (or to that of another business for the same time period). This is, however, a fairly obvious form of analysis that provides very little benefit or insight. Regrettably, not only is there nothing intrinsically enlightening about information based on an ordinal ranking scale, but this data could be subject to misinterpretation because of the inherent deficiencies attributable to the unit of currency.

In addition, although an assessment can be made of the comparative performance of any individual financial variable on an ordinal ranking basis, an accurate conclusion of the *significance* of any differences can only be made when the values are considered in relation to the relative size of operations of the respective businesses. Consequently, although such an approach may provide a legitimate basis for the comparison of *raw* performance, it offers a limited benefit when attempting to benchmark *relative* performance in instances where there are significant differences in the perspective scale of subjects under examination. It could be concluded that despite the ordinal classification system providing a marginal increase in utility over simple numerical values, it is not able to overcome the identified shortcomings for business financial performance measurement that currency possesses. Moreover, any gains that the ordinal scale may generate in terms of the comparability of information can be considered illusory, given the inability of this method to compensate for the phenomenon of perspective scale.

Interval currency changes

It was shown that the currency values of variables reported in financial statements have a lack of inherent context. In an attempt to overcome this and to try and create 'external' context (to the individual data values), the information within financial statements will customarily present the data for the most recent period, alongside the equivalent data, from the immediately preceding period. This is an attempt to provide 'internal' benchmarking capabilities for variable values that otherwise have no inherent qualitative capacity. An extension of this objective is the practice of ascertaining the magnitude of any change in the value of variables between the periods presented in financial statements and reporting these changes as 'variances'.

This provides a quick method to demonstrate the direction and quantity of a change in the value of a financial variable to assist the users of financial information to better understand the performance of that variable in the time frame being assessed.

Interval currency changes and inherent context

One of the main deficiencies of currency values for financial variables for the purpose of financial performance measurement is the lack of inherent context. The practice of determining currency value interval amounts over time advances on the practice of reporting currency values alone. This is because a value that represents an interval, or change, in the value of a variable will possess the characteristic of inherent context. An interval value will indicate (on its own) whether the value of a variable has increased or decreased and by how much. This demonstrates that currency interval values possess an inherent context.

Interval currency changes and currency translation

The assessment of the currency interval changes for the financial variables of an organisation will help to quantify the performance of those variables and the organisation. It will not, however, provide any assistance with qualitative assessments of that performance. If internal benchmarking is not sufficient to help achieve this objective, the search for external context and, therefore, some independent form of performance comparison could be sought from the financial information of other (usually similar) entities through the practice of external benchmarking. To illustrate this practice, the information that was contained in Table 2.1 for three professional bodies will be expanded to include the comparative 2009 year data for the same key financial variables.

One of the main reasons for selecting these three professional bodies for these examples is that they report their financial information in different currencies. This illustrates the issue of different currency 'scales' for the purposes of measurement. The numerical values for this combined information (in their natural currency scales) have been presented in a format that would be consistent with the traditional presentation of financial statements (Table 2.9). In order to assess the magnitude of the change for the listed variables between the two periods, the values from 2009 were deducted from the values in 2010. The results from this calculation are summarised in Table 2.10.

An analyst could compare the values in Table 2.10 to those in Table 2.9 for each organisation to assess the magnitude of the change for each variable in terms of currency units. This should provide an impression of whether the change was significant for each individual variable by comparing the change to the values of the variables used in the calculation. For example, the currency change of $12.974 million for the surplus of USPA (refer to

Table 2.9 Key financial data for three professional associations for two financial years[a]

Variable	USPA		UKPA		AUSPA	
	USD ('000)		GBP ('000)		AUD ('000)	
	2009	2010	2009	2010	2009	2010
Membership Fees	1,03,879	1,07,821	37,250	38,884	54,664	58,250
Surplus	−4,118	8,856	915	1089	3,548	11,807
Total Assets	2,32,050	2,25,663	31,957	33,057	84,501	95,164
Total Liabilities	2,01,922	1,77,312	21,379	20,867	47,722	46,844
Total Equity	30,128	48,351	10,578	12,190	36,779	48,320

a Obtained from 2010 Annual Reports (various).

Table 2.10 Currency variances for data in Table 2.9[a]

Variable	USPA	UKPA	AUSPA
	ΔUSD ('000)	ΔGBP ('000)	ΔAUD ('000)
Membership Fees	3,942	1,634	3,586
Surplus	12,974	174	8,259
Total Assets	−6,387	1,100	10,663
Total Liabilities	−24,610	−512	−878
Total Equity	18,223	1,612	11,541

a Calculated by deducting 2009 values in Table 2.9 from 2010 values in Table 2.9.

Table 2.10) was significantly greater (more than three times the size) than the 2009 result and much larger than the change from the 2010 result (nearly one and a half times the size). This is an example of 'internal' benchmarking for context. The calculations determined in this manner are simultaneously proportionally consistent with the variables the method was applied to and with all of the other variables that form the overall data set. In this way, the change for one variable can be compared to the changes in other variables to ascertain which changes were the most significant *for the organisation*.

Although this is helpful and can offer some insight into the financial performance of an organisation, the interval values themselves suffer from the same issues as the currency values they are derived from. An example of this is that values reported in different currencies need to be translated to enable a valid comparison, and it is known that the conversion rates for this practice are inconsistent. Consequently, if the values for the financial variables in Table 2.10 are compared among the different bodies, there can be no insight or conclusions made about the relative performance of those bodies because the values have not been translated into a common currency unit. For instance, although the change in Membership Fees of $3.942 million for USPA reported in Table 2.10 may be a similar raw number to the AU$ 3.586

million change for AUSPA in Table 2.10, it cannot actually be compared directly until one value is translated into the same currency unit as the value for the other entity.

Unfortunately, unlike other measurement scales, the rate of translation between different scales for the same object being measured is not constant. If, for example, the change in Membership Fees for AUSPA in Table 2.9 were converted into USD at the rate on 30 June 2010 (from Table 1.1), the value of the change in USD would be $3.065 million for AUSPA. If, however, the translation was made using the rate of exchange on 30 June 2011 (from Table 1.2), the value of the change for AUSPA would be $3.856 million. Quite clearly, an inconstant rate of conversion for different currencies is a major problem for currency-related measurement techniques. Given these issues, the list of changes for each professional body in Table 2.10 will only be of benefit if they are compared to the values from which they are derived or, alternatively, if they are compared to the changes for the other variables. On its own, the change in Membership Fees for UKPA of £1.634 million as reported in Table 2.10, for example, cannot impart any insight into the performance of that specific variable or for the organisation as a whole without further manipulation or comparison of the data.

Interval currency changes and perspective scale

Another other major problem for currency-related measurement techniques is that the comparison of the currency values of different variables and the changes in currency values between different organisations may be distorted by the influence of the phenomenon of perspective scale. In effect, what this means is that, regardless of whether currency values are able to be converted at a constant rate, the values for the same variables of different organisations may not be comparable anyway. As demonstrated in Chapter 1, there is a reasonable expectation that as a business grows in size, the numerical currency values of financial variables should grow proportionately. This means that although there may be numerical growth in the value of a financial variable, this growth may not be representative of a change in performance. In other words, the number may be *bigger* than a previous number, but it doesn't mean it was *better*.

The effect of perspective scale on the assessment of financial performance means that, even if the currency interval changes listed in Table 2.10 were converted at a constant rate of exchange, there can be no direct comparison of performance between organisations if the values have not been normalised in a manner that neutralises differences in operational size. For example, it could be that although the currency interval variances depicted for UKPA in Table 2.10 appear to be relatively insignificant (in comparison to the other two bodies), it may be that those variances are actually more significant than those they are benchmarked against once issues relating to currency and perspective scale have been neutralised. Because of the different currencies being utilised, not only can the variances not be directly compared between the businesses, but there is also an inability to ascertain the significance of any of the variances from this technique because of the influence of perspective scale.

Case study: review of interval currency changes analysis for GM

To determine the currency interval changes for GM for the financial year period 2009–2011, the changes in the values of the variables presented in Figure 2.1 were calculated by deducting the value of the earlier period from the value of the most recent period for each period of data. The values determined from this procedure for the information in this example are presented in Figure 2.2. The most obvious difference to the information presented in Figure 2.1 is that the first column in Figure 2.2 does not have any values for any of the variables. As such, there is no analytical insight for the first period of data when this method is applied in this way.

Representing the changes in the values of financial variables, the amounts reported in Figure 2.2 indicate the numerical size and direction of any change in the values of the variables being examined. There is, however, no expression of the *relative* magnitude of the change for any *individual* value without reference to the base values from which they were derived. Income, for example, is a critical aspect of the financial performance of any organisation and, therefore, of great interest. The Total Revenue figures for each individual period reported in Figure 2.1 are positive and sizeable. Apart from this conclusion, however, any insight into the quality of the performance of the variable is only revealed by the trend over the whole period of analysis. In other words, more than one period of data is required to appreciate the performance of any single value.

This situation has not been improved by identifying the interval change values for the Total Revenue variable reported in Figure 2.2. Although the changes in the value of variables across periods provide a value that indicates the size and direction of the change, the *relative* magnitude of the changes can only be appreciated by a direct comparison to the values involved in each calculation. It is for this reason that traditional 'variance reporting' is presented in the manner that it usually is (two columns of data followed by the variance). In order to appreciate the performance of Total Revenue for GM in the three years of analysis, all of the three values in Figure 2.1 for this variable are required in order to determine that the income for GM increased positively for each period and for the time frame overall.

While the interval currency changes in Figure 2.2 indicate positive changes in Total Revenue that are of sizeable values, the change for Total Revenue in 2011 of $14,853 million needs to be compared to the $30,834 million change experienced in 2010 in order to assess the relative performance of each period for *this* variable. Indeed, even the knowledge that Total Revenue

	2009 ΔUSD m	2010 ΔUSD m	2011 ΔUSD m
Trading Statement			
Revenue			
Automotive Sales	0	30,553	13,724
GM Financial Revenue	0	281	1,129
Total Revenue	0	30,834	14,853
Expenses			
Automotive Cost of Sales	0	6,638	11,618
GM Financial Expenses	0	152	633
Automotive Selling, General & Admin	0	-721	659
Other Automotive Expenses	0	-1,132	-60
Goodwill Impairment	0	0	1,286
Total Costs & Expenses	0	4,937	14,136
Operating Income /(Loss)	0	25,897	717
Balance Sheet			
Assets			
Automotive Current Assets	0	-6,194	7,194
Automotive Non-Current Assets	0	-2,135	-3,600
GM Financial Assets	0	10,932	2,111
Total Assets	0	2,603	5,705
Liabilities			
Automotive Current Liabilities	0	-5,278	1,775
Automotive Non-Current Liabilities	0	-7,682	637
GM Finance Liabilities	0	7,359	1,461
Total Liabilities	0	-5,601	3,873
Net Assets	0	8,204	1,832
Equity	0	8,204	1,832
Total Equity	0	8,204	1,832

Figure 2.2 Currency interval changes for GM[a].
a Obtained from the values in Figure 2.1.

increased by a larger value in 2010 than it did in 2011 does not automatically indicate that it was a *better* performance. This is the fundamental deficiency of an absence of an understanding of the perspective scale involved. A larger number from currency-based measurements does *not* automatically indicate better. Consider the values for the Total Costs and Expenses variable for GM for the time period examined. In a manner similar to the values for the Total Revenue variable, the values for Total Costs and Expenses increased in each period reported in Figure 2.1.

Unlike revenue, however, expenditure is considered a negative impost on wealth and, therefore, an increase in this variable is not considered positive. For this reason, the larger numerical increase in Total Costs and Expenses in 2011 of $14,136 million for GM would be considered a worse result than the $4,937 million in 2010 (refer to Figure 2.2). This is where the issue of *internal* perspective scale takes effect. The performance of Total Revenue cannot be examined in isolation of Total Costs and Expenses (using any currency-based measurement values), because any numerical changes in either variable may be a result in changes in the size of the business itself and not a consequence of changes in the efficiency and effectiveness of the variables being examined. Therefore, although the currency interval method enables a narrative to be formed about the relative performance of related variables over a series of periods, this system does not convey instantly whether any specific result for any individual variable is 'good' and nor to what extent.

Assessment of currency interval changes as a technique to measure financial performance

In terms of assisting the assessment of the performance of specific financial variables or, for an organisation overall, the currency interval technique provides some additional utility to stand-alone currency values. However, these values also suffer from all of the same issues that the currency stand-alone values suffer from and, consequently, are insufficient to achieve the objectives of financial performance assessment. The impact of perspective scale, for example, renders the currency interval scale technique incapable of assisting any assessment of *relative* performance when outcomes between businesses with different operational scales are compared against each other. This aspect makes it difficult to rely upon the outputs of the technique to enable valid comparisons among businesses of different operational scales and, subsequently, limits the usefulness of the methodology in benchmarking applications. The impact of perspective scale in relation to individual business performance can also affect the analysis of internal performance over time and within the same period. All of these issues combine to render the currency changes techniques as unable to adequately meet the needs of financial performance measurement and assessment.

Summary

The fundamental unit of measurement for financial reporting purposes is currency. All financial statements report the activities of a business using currency values. Unfortunately, currency is an inadequate unit of measurement as it is unable to overcome issues of inherent context, temporal consistency, inherent worth, consistent conversion and perspective scale. This chapter explored what these issues were and how, as a result of their influence, rendered currency an imperfect unit of measurement and any technique that relied on them to measure financial performance inadequate for purpose.

Conclusion for currency as a measurement unit

While inferences can be drawn about whether a financial value reported in currency values is higher or lower than another value, there is no objective way to determine which currency value is any better or worse than any other currency value. This general lack of utility is further compromised by the understanding that despite the numerical nature of currency, its value as a unit of measurement is severely compromised by its inability to maintain a constant level of inherent worth. It is also diminished by the lack of consistent conversion rates between different currency units. Ultimately, given that currency is the fundamental unit of measurement for nominal financial information, the identified deficiencies will affect any system that relies solely upon currency values to assess financial performance. The flaws that currency possesses as a unit of measurement include a lack of consistency (worth and conversion), comparability (worth and conversion) and, therefore, reliability.

References

AUSPA, 2010. CPA Australia Annual Report 2010.
GM, 2009. GM Annual Report 2009.
GM, 2010. GM Annual Report 2010.
GM, 2011. GM Annual Report 2011.
UKPA, 2010. CIMA Chartered Institute of Management Accountants, Financial Statements 2010.
USPA, 2010. AICPA American Institute of CPAs, Annual Report 2010.

3 Issues with percentages, ratios and other attempts at absolute measurement scales

Abstract

In many respects, the techniques that were examined in this chapter have been an improvement over currency-based analysis methodologies. Most of the techniques in this chapter, for example, were able to overcome issues of perspective scale and currency conversion. It is a result of benefits such as these that, as a consequence, ensure the percentage change technique is currently the most widely utilised means of conveying financial performance to interested parties. Despite the techniques of this chapter being an improvement on currency as a measurement scale, however, they are ultimately subject to their own deficiencies and, subsequently, will ultimately fall short of satisfying the needs of users and of being a quality measurement unit for the purposes of financial performance assessment.

Introduction

This chapter will explore some of the techniques that have been widely adopted because they rely on measurement scales that are more superior to the basic unit of currency. Unfortunately, while they may be better than currency for the purpose of measuring financial performance, even these techniques are subject to their own issues that ultimately render them inadequate for this purpose. The techniques that will be explored in this chapter are (i) the percentage change, (ii) ratios and (iii) horizontal trend analysis (HTA) and vertical ratio analysis (VRA).

Percentage changes

Although changes in the currency amount of a financial variable over time can *quantify* a change in performance, it remains unable to convey the *quality* of the performance. However, the process of determining the currency changes over time is not only an analytical method in itself, but also provides the basis required for the calculation of percentage changes. The outputs of the percentage change method are instantly recognised and understood by every possible user of the information. Consequently, there is a prolific tendency to ascertain the magnitude of change in the variables in financial statements by determining the percentage change in those variables. As such, every annual report and financial commentary in journals, newspapers and other media utilises this measure to convey the financial performance of different financial variables.

It should be further noted that percentage changes are actually a form of ratio. Indeed, it is some of the advantages of being a ratio that generates the widespread appeal to use this method. For instance, whereas a currency change for a financial variable of one business will rarely indicate the same magnitude of change for another business, a percentage change will be directly comparable between different businesses (irrespective of size).

Despite the simplicity and the mathematical integrity of the percentage change technique, however, there are a number of issues that render this method inadequate for the purposes of financial performance measurement and assessment. Importantly, it is rarely understood that the results are affected by two different factors utilised in the calculation. The first of these is the time frame being utilised for the analysis. The second is the size of the base value in comparison to the size of the change in variable value. The following discussion will examine each of these issues and their implications for the measurement and analysis of the financial performance of businesses.

Percentage changes and inherent context

In a similar vein to many other measurement scales for physical phenomenon, the mathematical percentage change technique has an element of inherent context. That is, anyone who is informed of a percentage change in a numerical value should instantly recognise the extent of the change by the number associated with the percentage descriptor. It would be difficult for an analyst, armed only with a currency change in the value of a variable, to ascertain the magnitude of the change in the value of that variable. On the other hand, a value that represents the percentage change in the amount of a variable should instantly convey the *magnitude* of the change in the value of the variable. This will indicate the change, or performance, of that specific variable for that specific period of time to the *base* value of that variable. This element is a major advancement over simple currency-only techniques.

This element of inherent context that a percentage change value possesses could be the main reason why it is such a popular technique for assessing and reporting financial performance. Unfortunately, although the percentage change technique ensures an element of inherent context that could assist users of that information in formulating opinions concerning financial performance, the value of this information is severely limited. The reason is that inherent context from the percentage change technique for an individual variable is only specific for that individual variable and becomes less beneficial in a larger data set. Furthermore, although the percentage change can quantify the size of the change in the value of a variable for a period of time, there are several factors (that will be explored in the following sections) that significantly diminish the utility of percentage change outputs.

Percentage changes and temporal consistency

One of the characteristics of a quality measurement scale that was reported in Chapter 1 is temporal consistency. This is an expectation that a measurement system should produce consistent outputs whether applied to short- or long-term periods of time. It is not the element of time itself that can influence the outcomes of a measurement system but, rather, the values of measurements from some methods can change depending solely upon the periods of time that were utilised in the measurement. It is not the amount, or value, assigned to a variable for one specific period of time that causes the issues. It is when there are multiple values for multiple periods of time that are being assessed where this issue will manifest.

The temporal inconsistency of the percentage change technique can be demonstrated with a very simple example. Table 3.1 contains a hypothetical sequence of profit results over a seven-year period and the associated annual percentage change values of those profit results. According to the results in Table 3.1, the percentage change result is *diminishing* over each period from 10 per cent in period 2 to 6.7 per cent in period 7. These results are determined by calculating the change of the value of the profit variable in one period from the value of the immediately preceding period. If, however, the time frame of the calculation was altered, the result determined in this example would also change. If, for example, the change in the value of profit in period 7 was compared to that in the value in period 1 and a percentage change was determined, then the resulting measurement would be 60 per cent.

The long-term calculation of 60 per cent provides a vastly different impression of performance than the one suggested by annual percentage change values. Indeed, if the long-term result of 60 per cent was averaged out in order to determine values per period, the result would be an average of 10 per cent per period. This is, again, contrary to the individual percentage change calculations and highlights that the percentage change methodology is incapable of being accurate *and* consistent over both short and long time frames. It is this lack of temporal consistency that renders the percentage change technique of financial performance measurement as inadequate for its intended purpose.

Table 3.1 Hypothetical profit sequence and percentage change from previous period

Time (t)	1	2	3	4	5	6	7
Profit (π)	100	110	120	130	140	150	160
% Change (%Δ)	–	10	9.1	8.3	7.7	7.1	6.7

Percentage changes and perspective scale

Not only does the percentage change method have mathematical integrity, it is also accepted that percentage changes have an element of inherent context. This provides an analyst with some insight into the magnitude of the change in a financial variable for a specific period of time. This measure also provides an avenue for analysts to externally benchmark performance against other organisations that may have a significant difference in perspective size. This is because a 50 per cent increase in the Surplus for an organisation that has Total Assets of $100,000 will equate to a 50 per cent increase in the Surplus for an organisation that has Total Assets of $200,000.

Unfortunately, however, any faith in the outputs of the percentage change methodology that is borne from the mathematical accuracy of single-period calculations could be completely misplaced. The responsibility for this can be pinpointed to the relationship that percentage change calculations have with the size, or scale, of the data being compared. This is the second major deficiency of the percentage change technique and is also ultimately responsible for the issue relating to the temporal inconsistency for the method. The underlying cause of this issue is the size of the base of each calculation. To illustrate this concept, consider the differences between the percentage change calculations of a $1 change compared to a base of $1 and then to a base of $100. Although the actual change of $1 would be the same in both cases, the outcome would be a 100 per cent variance for the $1 base and only a 1 per cent variance for the $100 base. Despite the numerical change being the same, the percentage calculations provide vastly different impressions of performance and, more importantly, the *significance* of the variance.

While this feature may ensure that the percentage change technique overcomes perspective-scale differences between organisations, it becomes the cause of an issue when the technique is applied internally. If the example of the change of one dollar was for the same variable for two different organisations, then the technique overcomes perspective scale. If, however, the changes were for two different variables in the same data set for an organisation, it becomes a problem. Although the percentage changes for the *individual* variables are mathematically valid, the change of one dollar will have the same significance for that *organisation* in both instances.

The perspective-scale influence of the base is not limited to the internal context issues of the previous example. It is also an issue that arises from instances where the value of one specific variable will increase over time. This situation results in every subsequent base value for comparison increasing and, consequently, will result in the percentage change calculation to diminish over time. As a consequence, this technique can produce results that may mislead an analyst when applied specifically to the purpose of assessing the financial performance of that variable and for an organisation overall.

The choice of the values in the hypothetical sequence of profits in Table 3.1 was made deliberately to enable a demonstration of this phenomenon. It

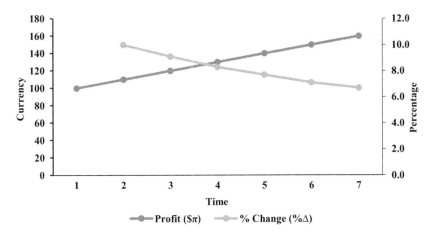

Figure 3.1 Profit currency value and percentage change in profit over time.

clearly demonstrates that although the periodical value for profit is increasing by a constant value of ten currency units per period, the periodical percentage change is decreasing from 10 per cent in period 2 to 6.7 per cent in period 7. Although the percentage change calculation for each period is mathematically correct, the impression of the trend of performance is diametrically opposed to the actual increases in the value of the profit variable over time (refer to Figure 3.1). It may be, in fact, that the short-term integrity of this technique could have unduly encouraged analysts to rely upon calculations that are limited to the two time periods traditionally contained within the reported financial statements.

Percentage changes and different currencies

In comparison to currency-only techniques, one of the major advantages of the percentage change technique is that it overcomes the issue of currency translation. This concept can be explored through an example. The data that will be used for this illustration will be based on information relating to the three professional bodies utilised previously (AUSPA, UKPA and USPA). The percentage changes for this example were determined using the currency interval changes in Table 2.10 and the values in Table 2.9 as the base for the calculations. The results of these calculations are summarised in Table 3.2.

The information in Tables 2.9 and 2.10 cannot be compared directly because the values presented in those tables are reported in different currency scales. The major advantage of the percentage change technique is that it is a form of ratio, and therefore, when the technique is applied to values of different currencies, the outputs of this technique will require no prior

Table 3.2 Percentage change variances over one-year time frame for professional bodies[a]

Variable	USPA	UKPA	AUSPA
	%Δ	%Δ	%Δ
Membership Fees	3.79	4.39	6.56
Surplus	−315.06	19.02	232.78
Total Assets	−2.75	3.44	12.62
Total Liabilities	−12.19	−2.39	−1.84
Total Equity	60.49	15.24	31.38

a Determined by dividing values in Table 2.10 over the 2009 base values in Table 2.9.

conversion of the currency values. As a result, the percentage change values presented in Table 3.2 can be compared directly to each other. Consequently, although there can be no comparative interpretations made for the relative performance of the currency interval changes in Table 2.10, the same cannot be said for the percentage change values in Table 3.2.

An example of this comparability is the results for the Membership Fees variable. It is noted that, in terms of the *percentage change* result, AUSPA reported the largest increase in 2010 for the Membership Fees variable of 6.56 per cent (refer to Table 3.2). Similarly, the percentage change values in Table 3.2 for the Total Equity variable indicate that the increase of 60.49 per cent for USPA was nearly twice the size of the result for AUSPA (31.38 per cent) and four times the result for UKPA (15.24 per cent). These are comparisons that can be made validly because the values being compared (unlike those currency values in Table 2.10) are reported in the same measurement scale.

While the percentage change technique overcomes the problem of comparability for values reported in different currencies, the ability to interpret the quality of the actual performance of the variables using this method is not straightforward. This is a result of the other issues associated with the percentage change technique. An example of these issues is that although the mathematical output of –315.06 per cent for the Surplus variable for USPA (refer to Table 3.2) indicates a disastrous result for the period, this was only a result of the base value being negative (a loss). The performance for USPA for the time frame of the analysis was actually *positive* because the variable went from a negative value to a positive value. For this variable, therefore, although USPA appears to be the worst-performing entity per the percentage change technique, it should actually be considered the best.

While the results reported in Table 3.2 reflect valid and accurate mathematical calculations for the variables being assessed, there are no *comparative* conclusions that can be made for any of these results because of internal context issues. Although a percentage change value for any specific variable may be of benefit *on its own* merit, it cannot provide any indication of significance or comparative performance when that single result is grouped

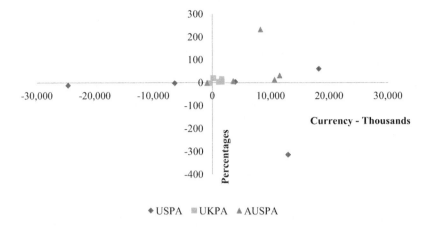

Figure 3.2 Currency and percentage changes in variables[a].
a Determined by dividing values in Figure 2.2 by base values in Figure 2.1.

with other values. As such, despite the possibility an analyst may be concerned (or pleased) about any *single* value in Table 3.2, there can be no direct comparison of performance that can be made for the variables within a single business, or for the same variable across different businesses. This is because the percentage change values have no direct correlation with the currency change values they were derived from when grouped with other values. This lack of correlation is depicted in Figure 3.2.

Case study: a percentage change analysis for GM

The percentage change technique is the most prolifically utilised technique to assess and report the performance of variables presented in financial statements. As such, the financial statement data for General Motors (GM) for the financial years ending 2009–2011 from previous analysis (refer to Figure 2.1) will also be utilised to demonstrate this method. The currency change data presented in Figure 2.2 was divided by the base values for the variables that were presented in Figure 2.1 in order to determine the percentage change values presented in Figure 3.3. In a similar way to the predicament that the currency interval change technique faces, the percentage change method has a necessity for a base period of data in order for an output to be determined. Consequently, the percentage change technique cannot provide any insight into the performance of any financial variable for the first period of analysis. This is apparent from the lack of any values in the column for the 2009 financial year for GM in Figure 3.3.

The issue of requiring a base value to enable calculations to be made is not limited to the first period of operation. This issue arises for *any* financial

	2009	2010	2011
	%Δ	%Δ	%Δ
Trading Statement			
Revenue			
Automotive Sales	–	29.21	10.16
GM Financial Revenue	–	ERR	401.78
Total Revenue	–	29.48	10.97
Expenses			
Automotive Cost of Sales	–	5.92	9.78
GM Financial Expenses	–	ERR	416.45
Automotive Selling, General & Admin	–	-5.93	5.76
Other Automotive Expenses	–	-90.56	-50.85
Goodwill Impairment	–	ERR	ERR
Total Costs & Expenses	–	3.93	10.83
Operating Income /(loss)	–	-123.57	14.52
Balance Sheet			
Assets			
Automotive Current Assets	–	-10.45	13.56
Automotive Non-Current Assets	–	-2.77	-4.81
GM Financial Assets	–	ERR	19.31
Total Assets	–	1.91	4.11
Liabilities			
Automotive Current Liabilities	–	-10.07	3.76
Automotive Non-Current Liabilities	–	-13.99	1.35
GM Finance Liabilities	–	ERR	19.85
Total Liabilities	–	-5.22	3.81
Net Assets	–	28.33	4.93
Equity	–	28.33	4.93
Total Equity	–	28.33	4.93

Figure 3.3 Percentage changes for GM (2009–2011)[a].
a Determined by dividing values in Figure 2.2 by base values in Figure 2.1.

variable in any period of analysis where the base value of the variable to be used in the calculation is a zero. This deficiency is the cause of the 'ERR' notation for five financial variables in the 2010 year column of Figure 3.3 (and for one variable in the 2011 column in Figure 3.3). An 'ERR' notation arises when a calculation is made in relation to variables with a zero base value. For each of these line items, a percentage change value could not be determined at all because the base value of these calculations for those variables was a zero. The inability of the percentage change technique to provide a value for any variable that has a zero base could mask a significant variation in performance (both positive and negative) that management may consequently miss. The 2010 'ERR' result for the GM Financial Assets variable in Figure 3.3 is a perfect example. The currency change for this variable for that time frame, per Figure 2.2, was $10,932 million (the most significant currency change for the balance sheet for that period) and couldn't register a percentage change value at all.

An inability to cope with a base value of zero is not the only major deficiency of the percentage change technique. An example of another issue arising from the value of a base figure can be found with the 2010 percentage change value for the 'Operating Income/(loss)' variable in Figure 3.3. On face value, the –123.57 per cent value for this variable (refer to Figure 3.3) would indicate that GM had a very poor change in their fortunes for the 2010 financial year. In reality, the currency change for this variable for that period was a *positive* $25,897 million (refer to Figure 2.2). The reason for this anomaly is that the base value for this particular example is a negative value and the negative output from a positive value change is a mathematical quirk of the percentage change technique.

This also leads to another major shortcoming of the percentage change methodology. Again, although the mathematical calculation itself is not questioned, the *significance* of a performance outcome for a financial variable could be understated or overstated drastically by the outcomes of a percentage change calculation. An example of this is the 2011 percentage change for the GM Financial Revenue variable in Figure 3.3. The percentage change for GM Financial Revenue for 2011 was 401.78 per cent (refer to Figure 3.3). The size of this value suggests that the change in the currency value for the variable must have been very significant for the *business* and should warrant further review. In fact, although the percentage change result *was* a very significant change for the *specific variable* it was calculated from, the actual currency change of $1,129 million was not a very significant factor to the overall performance of the *business*.

Assessment of percentage change measurement techniques

It is recognised that the percentage change methodology is the most widely utilised technique to convey the performance of financial variables to various stakeholders of organisations. This is most probably because the technique possesses a number of advantages over simple currency assessments of financial performance. For example, the percentage change technique allows an assessment of the order of magnitude of changes in the currency values of a financial variable. It also enables the direct comparison of the performance of the same variables between organisations that are trading in different currencies without the need for any currency conversion. Another positive aspect of this technique is that it also overcomes the influence or perspective scale when comparing entities of different operational sizes.

Despite the identified advantages and popularity of this method, however, the percentage change technique is subject to a number of deficiencies. This technique does not allow, for example, any calculations to be made for the first period of data. Similarly, this technique cannot produce any results where a base period value for a variable is zero. Furthermore, if the base value of a calculation is negative and the following value is positive, the percentage change will be mathematically negative despite the change actually being positive. Other disadvantages of the technique include a lack of temporal consistency and internal consistency (obscuring relative significance in a group of variables), and may produce results that can contradict the growth in a variable over time. Consequently, regardless of the advantages over currency-only techniques and despite the widespread acceptance and use of the technique, the disadvantages of the method outweigh its overall utility.

Ratios

The analysis of the financial performance of businesses requires the use of relative instruments that would enable valid direct comparisons between every business (and also in relation to the same business) over time. It is further noted that such an instrument could increase the level of confidence in the conclusions derived from the reviewed data. Unfortunately, there is an inability for currency (as a measurement unit) to adequately cope with comparisons of data using different currencies or different scales of operations over a number of different time periods. Consequently, to be successful, any potential alternative will need to overcome the issues with scale, time and context that beleaguer traditional measures. Regrettably, none of the techniques examined to date have been able to overcome all of the issues that were identified in Chapter 1. It is likely that the best solution to the problem of adequately measuring the financial performance of organisations will be some form of a ratio. This is because research norms dictate that although interval scales have superior characteristics to nominal and ordinal scales, ratio scales are '...the highest, most precise, level of measurement' (Gay and Diehl, 1992, pp. 152–153).

Ratio scales and inherent context

It was identified that percentage changes are a type of ratio and, therefore, have an element of inherent context. It is noted, consequently, that more formally acknowledged ratios will also possess this characteristic. So long as the variables utilised to determine a particular ratio are known to an analyst, a consumer of that information should instantly recognise the significance of the ratio value by its ratio descriptor. This element of inherent context is one of the characteristics that enable ratios to be a valuable tool for assessing, conveying and reporting financial performance. Despite this capability, however, the use of traditional ratios is restricted by the fact that they are generally limited to a few variables within a set of financial statements. As such, not every variable for which their performance may be of interest to an analyst can be assessed through the use of traditional ratios.

Ratio scales and temporal consistency

The characteristic of temporal consistency for a measurement scale or technique refers to the ability of that system to produce consistent results for both short- and long-term time frames. There is no doubt that a ratio technique will produce consistent results for short time frames because these scales will, generally, utilise variable values from the *same* period of time. The practice of applying financial ratios to the information in financial statements rarely considers how they could be applied to longer time frames. Temporal consistency for ratios as a financial measurement scale is, therefore, not an applicable issue in considering its efficacy in achieving its purpose.

Ratio scales and perspective scale

It is possible that because the percentage change technique provides a form of ratio, the phenomenon of perspective scale is not widely acknowledged as a benchmarking issue. It could be that the financial community believe that the percentage change technique already overcomes this specific issue. Evidence to support this notion could be construed from the prolific use of the percentage change technique in modern-day financial analysis. Regrettably, although it is a form of ratio, the percentage change technique has its own issues that it cannot overcome. Noting that the ideal business-benchmarking instrument would eliminate the impact of operational scale on the comparative analysis between businesses, the use of comparative ratios may be a better alternative.

Comparative ratios are those that are determined when the value of one variable is divided by the value of a *different* variable. This type of ratio will definitely provide *inherent* context. Such ratios that may be familiar include Return on Assets (ROA) and Net Margin ratios. A comparative ratio output is most valuable when it is compared to the output of another calculation (benchmarked). This comparison could be for the identical variables for the same business for a different period, or the same variables of another business for the identical period. This notion can be aided through a simple illustration. The example will utilise the variable of Income and compare it to the Total Assets variable to determine the income-generating capacity of the businesses. The information selected for this example is contained in Table 3.3. The data in Table 3.3 is for two hypothetical businesses (Firms A and B). The variables listed include the Income and Total Assets of the hypothetical businesses. Table 3.3 also reports the ratio of the Income to the Total Assets for each business.

Table 3.3 Hypothetical ratio comparison

Variable	Firm A	Firm B
Income	$50.00	$100.00
Total Assets	$100.00	$200.00
Income Ratio	0.50	0.50

In this example, in terms of the size of their Total Assets, one business (Firm B) is twice the size of Firm A (Total Assets of $200 compared to Total Assets of $100). This demonstrates the difference in perspective scale of the two businesses in the example. If the performance of the Income variable for the two businesses is compared on a numerical basis (currency values alone), it could be deduced that by generating a $50 greater level of income than Firm A, Firm B would be considered the better-performing business. The use of the ratio for this example, however, enables the relative disparity in size of the two businesses to be neutralised. Consequently, utilising the ratio analysis to eliminate the difference in size will enable a comparison of their performance in generating income on an 'equal' basis. The results from the application of a ratio technique to this information (0.50 for both Firms in Table 3.3) indicate that although the numerical currency values are disparate, the ratio values demonstrate that they *comparatively* performed exactly the same.

Ratio scales and different currencies

One of the shortcomings of currency as a measurement unit for the purpose of financial performance assessment is that the conversion rates between different currencies are not constant. This problem is not an issue for ratios because they do not need to convert the currency values of variables into a uniform currency in order to be utilised. For example, a ratio can be applied to a business operating in US currency (USD) and to a business that is operating in Australian currency (AUD), and the resulting values can be compared without any need for any conversion between the two forms of currency. The ability to overcome this deficiency can be illustrated with an example. The ratio employed for this example is the Net Margin ratio that is defined by Equation 3.1. This equation was applied to the information for the three professional bodies that were used in previous examples and contained in Table 2.9. The outputs of these calculations for this information are depicted in Figure 3.4.

Net margin ratio equation

$$\text{Net Margin Ratio} = (\text{Net Profit/Revenue}) \tag{3.1}$$

To illustrate the use of Equation 3.1, the Net Margin (Profit) and Revenue results for 2010 for the three professional organisations from Table 2.9 were utilised to provide the following outcomes:

$$AUSPA = (11,807 / 58,250) = 0.20$$
$$UKPA = (1,089 / 38,884) = 0.03$$
$$USPA = (8,856 / 107,821) = 0.08$$

Figure 3.4　Example calculations of Equation 3.1.

In order to assess which of the ratio outcomes in Figure 3.4 was the 'best' result, those outputs were ranked in order of largest-to-smallest (on the assumption that the larger the value, the better the result) and reported in Table 3.4. Unlike the ranking order of the results reported in Table 2.2, the order in Table 3.4 is actually meaningful. There are a number of reasons for this. The first is that the values in Table 3.4 are measured in the same scale (ratio scale) without the need for prior translation. The second is that, being a ratio output, the values have an inherent context (the number is an outcome of the relationship between two known variables). The last reason is that there is no influence of the phenomenon of perspective scale on the values that are being assessed.

As a result of these benefits, any conclusions about which result represented a better performance in this instance can be made validly. If the words of Gay and Diehl (1992) are considered, the result of the second ranked organisation in Table 2.2 (USPA) cannot (because of the different currencies) be validly described as more than eight times the size of the result of the next ranked organisation (UKPA) but, for the ratio results, however, the Net Margin result for USPA in Table 3.4 *can* be described as 2.67 times the size of the next placed result of UKPA. This is because the ratio scale utilised in Table 3.4 is superior to the currency scale used in Table 2.2 and allows this conclusion to be made. This is one of the most valuable advantages of a ratio scale.

Table 3.4　Ordinal ranking of Net Margin Ratio (NMR) from largest-to-smallest

Ordinal ranking	Organisation	Net margin Ratio
1	AUSPA	0.2
2	USPA	0.08
3	UKPA	0.03

Case study: ratio-scale assessment of the financial performance of GM

The financial statement values for GM for the financial years 2009–2011 (as reported in Figure 2.1) will assist the illustration of the use of ratio-scale measurement for financial performance analysis. This case study will utilise the ordinal ranking system in order to report the outputs of the application of ratio techniques in order of implied performance. Employing the Net Margin ratio (as used in Figure 3.4) on the data from Figure 2.1 (and presented on an ordinal ranking basis of largest-to-smallest), the ratios for the three years of financial information being assessed for GM are reported in Table 3.5.

The application of this particular ratio technique (Net Margin ratio), as reported in Table 3.5, has not changed the order of ranked performances from the order of the currency value surpluses reported in Table 2.7. This does not mean that the use of ratios in this analysis was subsequently void of any additional utility. While it is true, for example, that the 2011 currency value surplus was ranked on an ordinal basis above the result for 2010 because it was numerically 'bigger', it could not be deemed (on a prima-facie basis) to be 'better' than the other results, because the income from which it was derived was larger than that of the previous year. That is, it could be expected that more revenue would most likely provide a larger surplus if everything else changed in equal proportions.

Indeed, while the quality of the performance of the currency values for the surplus variable could not be comparatively assessed without additional information, the normalisation of the currency values to their respective (and perspective) income allows a more supportable conclusion to be made. The use of the Net Margin ratio in this example eliminates the influence of perspective scale and, consequently, an analyst can confidently conclude that the 2011 year *was* the best-performing year for *this* metric based purely on a comparison of the ratio output numbers being assessed. In this case, for example, the quality of the 2011 performance can be quantified as being 0.0011 *better* than the 2010 result (by virtue of the Net Margin ratio outcome in 2011 being 0.0011 larger than 2010 in Table 3.5).

Table 3.5 Ordinal ranking of GM net margin ratio (NMR) for financial years 2009–2011 from largest-to-smallest[a]

Ordinal ranking	Financial year	NMR
1	2011	0.0376
2	2010	0.0365
3	2009	−0.2

a Data obtained from Figure 2.1.

Assessment of ratio-scale financial performance measurement techniques

In the same way as the percentage change technique, ratios overcome issues of perspective scale and the need for currency conversion. Because they are performed on data for the same period, ratios are also temporally consistent and enable values to be determined for the first period of available data. Furthermore, ratios do not have mathematical calculation issues in situations where there are negative values involved. Ratios are, therefore, superior to percentage change and currency as a scale for the measurement of financial performance. Despite this, a limiting disadvantage of most ratios is that they are usually determined for a limited number of variables. An example of a variable-specific ratio is the Net Margin ratio. Another example is the Gross Profit ratio. Although ratios enable superior levels of benchmarking and also overcome many of the issues of percentage change and currency-based techniques, this aspect of only assessing the performance of a specific relationship between two variables severely limits the level of their utility.

Previous efforts at an absolute scale

Although the ratio scale is recognised as a superior form of measurement for financial performance purposes, it has been shown that even these can fall short of the characteristics possessed by absolute scales (Gay and Diehl, 1992; Pike and Roos, 2007). An absolute scale is structured such that all properties of the scale reflect the attribute of what is being measured (Pike and Roos, 2007, p. 231). Of the existing financial performance measurement techniques that are widely known, the closest to achieving the status of an absolute scale for Business Financial Performance Measurement (BFPM) purposes include the little known 'vertical' and 'horizontal trend' methodologies. The following will not only examine the positive characteristics of these techniques, but also explore the deficiencies they possess that result in them ultimately falling short of being an ideal solution.

Horizontal trend analysis

The aim of the HTA technique is to focus on the trends over time of the financial statement variables being reviewed. There are two different approaches to this methodology. The first is identical to the percentage change techniques examined previously and is referred to as the rolling period-to-period HTA technique. Another application of the method is to tie, or 'anchor', the calculation of future variable values to the value of an initial base period. The major difference from the rolling period-to-period application is that the base period does not have to be the immediately preceding period – no matter how many periods into the future the analysis may be. Although this may appear to be a very minor modification to the traditional application of the percentage change methodology, it is actually a change of significant impact. This aspect will be examined in the sections that follow.

Horizontal trend analysis and inherent context

Similar to the percentage change methodology, the HTA approach produces a form of ratio. As a result, the outputs of the HTA technique will possess the characteristic of inherent context. One of the advantages of the HTA approach over the use of comparative ratios is that every value in a financial statement will have an inherent context that relates to the same variable from which they were derived and to which the context arises. The context that they arise from is their base period values. Noting that the design of comparative ratios will result in most financial variables not being considered as part of the analysis, this aspect initially appears to be a significant advantage for techniques such as the HTA method. Unfortunately, however, because a financial variable is only one value in a larger data set, the value of this context is, in a similar manner to the percentage change approach, extremely limited.

Horizontal trend analysis and perspective scale

It is noted that the rolling period-to-period version of HTA is exactly the same as the percentage change method. As a result, all of the benefits and shortcomings in relation to perspective scale that are applicable to the percentage change technique will also apply to the rolling period-to-period version of HTA. Although the anchored version of HTA is different in application and will be applied to multiple periods of time, the difference in the application of this technique is insufficient to overcome the same negative characteristics that the percentage change and rolling period-to-period application of HTA possess in regard to the issue of perspective scale.

Horizontal trend analysis and temporal consistency

Again, as the rolling period-to-period application of HTA is identical to the percentage change technique, all of the same issues concerning its lack of temporal consistency will also apply to the rolling period-to-period version of this method. The limitation of temporal inconsistency for the rolling period-to-period technique arises from determining the calculations for successive periods in isolation of the other values over time. In comparison to the contra-indicatory nature of the results from the rolling period-to-period application, the calculations made using the anchored version of the HTA method will more accurately portray performance over longer time frames. This is because the potential to influence the outcomes by results that may occur between calculations will be ignored by the results generated by the anchored version of HTA. The temporal abilities of the anchored

Table 3.6 Hypothetical profit sequence and anchored horizontal ratio changes

Time (t)	1	2	3	4	5	6	7
Profit ($?)	100	110	120	130	140	150	160
Horizontal change (%?)	–	10	20	30	40	50	60

version of HTA can be illustrated through the use of an example. For this purpose, the anchored version of the HTA technique will be applied to the same hypothetical profit sequence that was reported in Table 3.5 for the rolling period-to-period (percentage change) application.

The application of the anchored HTA method to the information in this example involved selecting the $100 profit for the first period to act as the base for all future calculations to be anchored against. The resulting percentages of this process are labelled in Table 3.6 as 'horizontal change (%Δ)'. The major difference between the horizontal change values in Table 3.6 and those from Table 3.5 is that the values in this application are increasing over time in the same direction as the currency values from which they are derived. When, for any individual period in Table 3.6, the horizontal change value is compared to the currency change for the profit variable from the base currency value, for the same period of time, the horizontal change will match the currency change for the same period. This ensures that the technique has a temporal consistency whether the calculation is for a short or long period of time.

Horizontal trend analysis and currency translation

One of the major advantages of the percentage change technique is that it overcomes the issue of currency translation. An example of how this is achieved is provided in Table 3.2. As the rolling-period-to-period version of HTA is identical to the percentage change technique, this method will also possess the same ability to overcome the comparison of data presented in different currency units. Although the anchored version of HTA has a different application to the rolling period-to-period version, it will, nevertheless, also possess the identical ability to enable the comparison of data presented in different currency units without prior translation.

Case study: horizontal trend analysis (rolling period-to-period) for GM

The previous use of the data from the financial reports of GM (refer to Figure 2.1) to illustrate financial performance measurement techniques will continue for the HTA methodology. The application of the HTA technique to the data listed in Figure 2.1 can be performed utilising either of two different approaches. The first version that will be reviewed is the *rolling period-to-period* method. This approach determines the percentage change in the value of a variable in one period in relation to the value of the variable in prior periods on a rolling period-to-period basis. When applied to the variable values for GM in Figure 2.1, the results from this technique will be identical to those from the traditional percentage change methodology (which is illustrated in Figure 3.3). As a result, there is no need for additional analysis and commentary to that which was provided for the GM case study in that section.

Case study: horizontal trend analysis (anchored) for GM

The second method of applying the HTA technique involves comparing every future period of information to the values of the same variable from an arbitrarily selected base period – no matter how many periods into the future the analysis may be. The application of the anchored HTA methodology to data for GM contained in Figure 2.1 results in the values reported in Figure 3.5. The most noticeable feature of the information contained in Figure 3.5 is that, until the 2011 financial year, the values calculated with the anchored version of the anchored HTA technique are *identical* to those determined by the rolling period-to-period version in Figure 3.3. For the anchored version of the technique, however, any results subsequent to the 2010 financial year (2011 and beyond) will be calculated as though there were no intervening time periods following the base period.

This raises the first shortcoming of the anchored version of HTA. Despite the source information for the analysis presented in Figure 2.1 being for three financial years, the most obvious outcome of the anchored application of HTA as presented in Figure 3.6 is that there are no values listed at all for the financial year ending 2009. This is a fundamental deficiency of both the percentage change and rolling period-to-period HTA techniques, and occurs because of an absence of any comparative data for the first period of any analysis. This will inevitably result in any calculations for the base period not being possible.

In the percentage change analysis and rolling period-to-period application of the HTA (Figure 3.3) to the data in Figure 2.1, there were five instances in the 2010 period and only one instance in the 2011 period where, because of a zero in the base value of the calculation, there was no calculation possible (ERR values). However, given that the first period of information becomes the base period for *all* subsequent periods in the anchored HTA version, the 2011 period for this technique has five instances (refer to Figure 3.5) where a calculation could not be made (ERR) because the first period's base value was a zero. This will occur even if the variables being assessed have values for the periods in between the base period and the period being assessed.

Another problem that becomes a compounding issue for this technique is that, in a manner that is similar to instances where the base value is a zero,

	2009	2010	2011
	%	%	%
Trading Statement			
Revenue			
Automotive Sales	0	29.21	42.33
GM Financial Revenue	0	ERR	ERR
Total Revenue	0	29.48	43.68
Expenses			
Automotive Cost of Sales	0	5.92	16.28
GM Financial Expenses	0	ERR	ERR
Automotive Selling, General & Admin	0	-5.93	-0.51
Other Automotive Expenses	0	-90.56	-95.36
Goodwill Impairment	0	ERR	ERR
Total Costs & Expenses	0	3.93	15.19
Operating Income / (loss)	0	-123.57	-126.99
Balance Sheet			
Assets			
Automotive Current Assets	0	-10.45	1.69
Automotive Non-Current Assets	0	-2.77	-7.44
GM Financial Assets	0	ERR	ERR
Total Assets	0	1.91	6.1
Liabilities			
Automotive Current Liabilities	0	-10.07	-6.68
Automotive Non-Current Liabilities	0	-13.99	-12.83
GM Finance Liabilities	0	ERR	ERR
Total Liabilities	0	-5.22	-1.61
Net Assets	0	28.33	34.66
Equity	0	28.33	34.66
Total Equity	0	28.33	34.66

Figure 3.5 Anchored HTA for GM (2009–2011)[a].
a   Determined by calculating the changes in variables to their 2009 value in Figure 2.1 and dividing it by that base value.

any negative values for the base period will also affect all future assessments regardless of intervening data values. The best example of this are the anchored HTA values for the Operating Income/(loss) variable for GM in Figure 3.5. Whereas the percentage change method only has one incorrectly negative result for the Operating Income/(loss) variable in 2010 (as per

Figure 3.3), the anchored HTA also has an incorrectly negative value for the 2011 year (refer to Figure 3.5).

A good example of how the anchored HTA method is meant to operate is the Automotive Sales values for GM. If the period-to-period approach to the HTA methodology is applied to the data in Figure 2.1, then the change in the values for the Automotive Sales variable for GM would be 10.16 per cent for the 2011 financial year (refer to Figure 3.3). This differs from the value of 42.33 per cent for the Automotive Sales variable for GM for 2011 determined by the alternative anchored version of the HTA technique (refer to Figure 3.5).

Noting that this value was calculated in comparison to the 2009 financial year, the anchored 2011 value represents a change that has occurred over a time frame of two years instead of the standard one. If this is taken into account, the average performance of the Automotive Sales variable for GM over the two-year time frame of just over 21 per cent was still higher than the standard rolling period version of the methodology. Alternatively, if the 2010 value were to be deducted from the 2011 calculation (from Figure 3.5), then the outcome of 13.12 per cent would still exceed the 2011 value from the rolling technique.

Assessment of the horizontal trend analysis methodology

Given that it is, in essence, another version of the percentage change methodology, all of the advantages and disadvantages of that method also apply to the rolling period-to-period version of the HTA technique. As such, this section will focus more on the alternative version of the HTA methodology where calculations are anchored to the values in a base period. It is noted, for instance, that the anchored version possesses an improved temporal consistency over that exhibited by the rolling version. Indeed, the anchored HTA technique provides outcomes that do not contradict the actual data, simply because of variations in the selected analytical time frame.

Despite this, the usefulness of the anchored version of the HTA methodology is erased in instances where base period variables are non-existent or have a zero value. In such instances, any calculation for *every* period that succeeds the base period would not be possible. Furthermore, while the anchored HTA technique overcomes the issues faced by the percentage change technique related to temporal consistency, the HTA methodology remains incapable of eliminating the issue of internal inconsistencies of scale variations *between* variables. Although not specifically mentioned by them, Siegel and Shim (2006, p. 240) referred to this problem with the statement that '...it is essential to present both the dollar amount of change and the percentage of change, since either one alone might be misleading...'. It can, therefore, be concluded that despite some of the benefits of the anchored HTA technique, the negative issues that can be attributed to this methodology combine to render the technique unable to satisfy the needs of users in terms of financial performance measurement and analysis.

Vertical ratio analysis

The previously reviewed HTA technique examines how the values of financial variables change over time. The VRA technique, however, examines the proportional relativity of the individual variables in a collection, to the variable of *largest* value in that collection, for a single period of time. In essence, the VRA methodology involves the conversion of the currency values of variables in a particular financial statement to ratios of the currency value of the variable with the largest balance within that same statement. This would typically involve comparisons to the Total Asset value for the analysis of balance sheet variables and to the Total Revenue variable for the analysis of the variables reported in a trading statement. Although the Total Revenue variable is assumed to possess the largest value of those reported in a trading statement, there will be many instances where this will not be the case. Not only will there be examples where the revenue for a period is not the largest value, there may, in fact, be occasions where there is no revenue whatsoever.

Vertical ratio analysis and inherent context

The outputs of the VRA methodology are ratios. As a result, they possess the characteristic of an inherent context where it is known that one variable has been assessed in direct relation to another variable. For this technique, the outputs for variables within the balance sheet will all have an inherent context to the Total Assets variable. This allows an instant appreciation of the significance of the values for those variables for that specific organisation. The treatment for the variables in the financial statement for this technique is slightly different. Although the variables in the financial statement will also have a base variable from which they were derived, the calculations for different periods may not have been made consistently against the same variable. As a result, although the outputs for the trading statement will have an inherent context, they may not be directly comparable to outputs from other time periods because of a possible inconsistency.

Vertical ratio analysis and perspective scale

Acknowledging that the outputs of the VRA method are ratios, these values would possess all of the identical characteristics of ratios that were identified in previous sections. As such, it is understood that the VRA outputs will assist to neutralise the phenomenon of perspective scale in benchmarking assessments. Because a ratio output is determined by the values of two variables within one data set, the output for the same ratio for a different organisations' data set will be directly comparable. The process of determining ratio values will overcome issues of perspective scale, and therefore, the VRA method will also be able to overcome this issue.

Vertical ratio analysis and temporal consistency

The VRA methodology is applied to the variables contained within the data set for one specific time period. As a result of this, the values that are determined through this technique will always be temporally consistent. Unfortunately, what this also means is that, because the technique does not assess performances across periods, this method cannot be used to ascertain any trends of numerical growth (as opposed to organic/holistic growth).

Vertical ratio analysis and currency translation

It was shown in previous sections that a ratio is a method by which the need to translate currency values to a consistent currency scale is eliminated. Noting that the VRA generates ratios, this aspect of its capabilities will be explored in this section. Subsequently, the VRA technique was applied to the information for the professional bodies examined in Chapter 2 and involved converting the information from Table 2.1 into vertical ratio outputs by dividing the currency value of each variable by the value of the largest variable in each financial statement. The values resulting from this process are reported in Table 3.7.

The application of the VRA method to the data in Table 2.1 required no currency translation of any of the variables in this example. Despite this, the converted values for each organisation in the example are now directly comparable to each other because they are all reported in the same scale of a vertical ratio output. The trading variable values in this example have been converted into ratios of the largest variable within the trading statement (of the available information in Table 2.1). In this case, the selected base variable for each organisation was Fee Income. As the base trading variable for this example was consistent for all three bodies, the ratio outputs for Fee Income were the same value of 1.0 (refer to Table 3.7). While this overcomes the phenomenon of perspective scale and renders the trading variable values

Table 3.7 Vertical Ratio values for key financial data for professional associations for 2010

Variable	USPA	UKPA	AUSPA
	USD	GBP	AUD
	('000)	('000)	('000)
Fee Income	1.00	1.00	1.00
Surplus	0.08	0.03	0.20
Total Assets	1.00	1.00	1.00
Total Liabilities	0.79	0.63	0.49
Total Equity	0.21	0.37	0.51

directly comparable, there is no insight that can be gained from the Fee Income variable itself.

The comparisons between the organisations for the Surplus variable are, however, more valuable. As a result of the normalisation process from the vertical ratio technique, valid direct comparisons between the associations can be made for the Surplus variable. It can be instantly ascertained, for example, that the VRA value for the Surplus variable for AUSPA is (at 0.20 per Table 3.7) the largest result for this variable among the three bodies. It is noted that this particular variable ratio output is exactly the same as would be generated by the Net Margin ratio equation and is widely utilised in the analysis of the financial performance of firms and organisations. Unlike this specific example, however, where there is only one additional trading variable in the data set to compare to Total Revenue, the application of VRA will be applied to many more variables than the single variable for the Net Margin ratio.

The application of the VRA technique to the balance sheet variables will provide better insight than those determined for the trading statement (as there are more variables for this example). The VRA technique normalises (makes all the businesses the same size) the Total Assets to values of 1.0 (refer to Table 3.7). Once the values in the balance sheet for each organisation have been normalised, the different variables can be validly directly compared to each other. For example, it can now be confidently concluded that the information in Table 3.7 showing the proportion between Total Liabilities and Total Equity for AUSPA is markedly different from the other two associations. It is noted that the Total Liabilities value for AUSPA is (at 0.49 from Table 3.7) less than half of its Total Asset value. This varies dramatically from the other two organisations for which their Liabilities ratio is close to, or greater than, twice the size of their Total Equity ratio.

It needs to be remembered that, for this example, the Total Liabilities for these organisations is predominantly represented by the unused portions of Membership Fees. Noting that the members do not actually own any equity in these bodies, the fact that Total Equity represents greater than half the proportion of Total Assets for AUSPA indicates significant retention of surpluses over time. This demonstrates that this type of analysis creates insight that allows questions to be asked, or examined, that may otherwise have not been thought of when utilising other techniques.

This result, for example, could lead to a more thorough review of the annual report for insight into the strategic direction of the different bodies. Having said that, there are some limitations to the insights available from the VRA methodology that arise from the application of the technique to the trading statement. There is, for example, no way of comparing the relative performance between the three organisations in their ability to generate revenue when the ratio for their Fee Income is the same value of 1.0 (refer to Table 3.7).

Case study: a vertical ratio analysis of GM

The financial statement values for GM for the financial years 2009–2011 as reported in Figure 2.1 will assist the illustration of VRA for financial performance analysis. The VRA methodology was applied to the data for GM within Figure 2.1, and the results are summarised in Figure 3.6. Unlike some of the other techniques examined to date, such as the HTA methodology, the VRA methodology is able to provide results for the first period of an analysis because the VRA is applied to the data of a specific period independently from any other period.

The governing rule of VRA is to utilise the variable with the largest value in a financial statement to form the base of the calculations for that statement. The balance sheet variable to be selected for the GM case study is a straightforward selection. In each year of data for this example, the Total Assets variable possesses the largest value in the balance sheet (refer to Figure 2.1). For this reason, the Total Assets variable was chosen as the base value for calculating the ratio for every balance sheet variable for every year of data in this example. Given that the Total Assets variable can be used consistently as the basis for the balance sheet calculations in this example, the results for the whole three financial years in the case study can be compared directly. For example, GM's Financial Assets has shown real growth in the balance sheet from 0.00 to 9.02 per cent of Total Assets over the time frame of analysis (refer to Figure 3.6). This is a conclusion that is not complicated by alternating base variables and is consequently totally reliable.

The situation for the trading statement for this example is, however, a more complicated issue. Although the Total Revenue variable has the largest value in the trading statement for 2010 and 2011, it is the Total Expenses variable that has the largest value for GM in 2009 (refer to Figure 2.1). This illustrates the first flaw in the VRA methodology as it is espoused. Noting that the governing rule for VRA is to utilise the variable in a financial statement with the largest value as the base for ratio calculations, the Total Costs & Expenses variable was selected as the trading statement base for 2009 as it possessed the largest value for that financial year in the trading statement (refer to Figure 2.1). As a result of this situation, the Total Costs & Expenses variable in 2009 generated the value of 100.00 (refer to Figure 3.6), and all of the other VRA values for that year were determined using this variable as a base. For the other two periods, however, the Total Revenue variable was selected as the base variable for the VRA calculations as they possessed the largest values in the trading statement for the 2010 and 2011 financial years (refer to Figure 2.1). Consequently, the VRA value for the Total Revenue variable for those years was 100.00 (refer to Figure 3.6), and all of the other VRA values for those years were determined using this variable as a base.

As a result of this simple inconsistency, none of the values determined for the trading statement in 2009 are in any way comparable to those for 2010 and 2011. This limits any insights and conclusions that can be drawn from this form of analysis for the trading statement for GM during the period of analysis. To overcome this issue, it could be argued that the Total Revenue variable should always be the base variable for trading statement calculations. Despite this, however, although this assumes that the Revenue

		2009 %	2010 %	2011 %
Trading Statement				
Revenue				
Automotive Sales		83.31	99.79	99.06
GM Financial Revenue		0	0.21	0.94
	Total Revenue	83.31	100	100
Expenses				
Automotive Cost of Sales		89.31	87.7	86.76
GM Financial Expenses		0	0.11	0.52
Automotive Selling, General & Admin		9.69	8.45	8.06
Other Automotive Expenses		1	0.09	0.04
Goodwill Impairment		0	0	0.86
	Total Costs & Expenses	100	96.35	96.24
	Operating Income / (loss)	-16.69	3.65	3.76
Balance Sheet				
Assets				
Automotive Current Assets		43.47	38.2	41.66
Automotive Non-Current Assets		56.53	53.93	49.32
GM Financial Assets		0	7.87	9.02
	Total Assets	100	100	100
Liabilities				
Automotive Current Liabilities		38.47	33.95	33.84
Automotive Non-Current Liabilities		40.28	34	33.1
GM Finance Liabilities		0	5.3	6.1
	Total Liabilities	78.76	73.25	73.04
	Net Assets	21.24	26.75	26.96
Equity		21.24	26.75	26.96
	Total Equity	21.24	26.75	26.96

Figure 3.6 A vertical ratio analysis of GM (2009–2011)[a].
a Determined by applying VRA to the values in Figure 2.1 to the Total Assets values for the balance sheet and the Total Expenses and Total Revenue variables in the trading statement as the base values.

variable is the largest value of those reported in a trading statement, there will be many instances where this will not be the case. Not only will there be instances where the revenue for a period is *not* the largest value, there may actually be occasions where these is no revenue whatsoever.

The unreliability of the Revenue variable (or any variable in the trading statement for that matter) to always possess the largest value will cause the resulting application of the VRA method to be inconsistent over time. This inconsistency is not only a problem in terms of the comparability of those specific variables over time, but for the comparability of *all* of the variables over time. The other main drawback of having a variable to be the base of trading statement calculations is that when the method is applied to the base variable, the outcome will always be a value of one. This means that there can be no insight for that specific variable. As the Total Assets variable will be the base variable for the balance sheet application of VRA, this variable will also be subject to the same drawback.

Assessment of the vertical ratio analysis methodology

It is accepted that the VRA treatment of the variables contained within the balance sheet of businesses will genuinely satisfy all of the characteristics of a quality measurement scale (including the internal and external validity of comparisons) in most instances. Even in these statements, however, there may be instances where the Total Liabilities will exceed the Total Assets and, consequently, the Total Assets variable will not be the largest variable in the balance sheet. This can become a problem for consistency over a number of different periods and for external benchmarking applications. The issue is amplified for the application of the VRA method to the information in trading statements. The comparison of trading statement variables to the Total Revenue variable will result in the calculations for the trading statement being non-comparable to the calculations made for the balance sheet for the same business, let alone if compared to those for other businesses. Furthermore, the linkage to the Total Revenue variable would only work for those businesses that actually have revenue, or this variable is significant enough that it is larger than all of the other variables in the statement.

If financial statement calculations that utilise this method are not consistently applied to the same variable over time, then issues of internal and external comparability diminish the usefulness of the information calculated. Apart from the possibility of an inconsistent base variable selection with this method, there is also a fundamental problem associated with predominantly selecting the revenue variable to form the base for trading statement calculations. This deficiency arises from the fact that the ratio calculation for any variable that is selected to form the base value for VRA will *always* be 100 per cent (or one). This inherent characteristic not only makes it impossible to ascertain the performance of the selected base variable over time but also incomparable to the performances of other businesses. Given this and recognising that it is one of the most important indicators of business performance, it would consequently be highly undesirable for any form of revenue to be selected as the base value for this type of analysis.

Summary

In many respects, the techniques that were examined in this chapter have been an improvement over currency-based analysis methodologies. Most of the techniques in this chapter, for example, were able to overcome issues of perspective scale and currency conversion. It is a result of benefits such as these that, as a consequence, ensure the percentage change technique is currently the most widely utilised means of conveying financial performance to interested parties. Despite the techniques of this chapter being an improvement on currency as a measurement scale, however, they are ultimately subject to their own deficiencies and, subsequently, will ultimately fall short of satisfying the needs of users and of being a quality measurement unit for the purposes of financial performance assessment.

References

AUSPA, 2010. CPA Australia Annual Report 2010.

Gay, L. and Diehl, P., 1992. *Research Methods for Business and Management.* New York: Macmillan Publishing Company.

GM, 2009. GM Annual Report 2009.

GM, 2010. GM Annual Report 2010.

GM, 2011. GM Annual Report 2011.

Pike, S. and Roos, G., 2007. The Validity of Measurement Frameworks. In: A. Neely, ed. *Business Performance Measurement: Unifying Theories and Integrating Practices.* Cambridge: Cambridge University Press, pp. 218–237.

Siegel, J.G. and Shim, J.K. (2006). *Accounting Handbook* (4th ed.). New York: Kaplan Publishing Attn, Barron's Educational Series, Inc.

UKPA, 2010. CIMA Chartered Institute of Management Accountants, Financial Statements 2010.

USPA, 2010. AICPA American Institute of CPAs, Annual Report 2010.

4 The proportional asset ratio (PAR) as a solution

Abstract

In an advancement from the VRA methodology, the proportional asset ratio (PAR) technique proposes the use of a single variable in the balance sheet (Total Assets) to form the base for ratio calculations of all of the variables in both financial statements. This was shown to overcome the problems encountered by the VRA method that arise from selecting a variable each for the balance sheet and trading statement to enable calculations. This chapter also demonstrated how the PAR technique overcomes other issues raised in Chapter 1, such as perspective scale, currency translation, context and temporal consistency. In short, this technique meets all of the characteristics of an absolute measurement scale for financial performance measurement, analysis and benchmarking.

Introduction

Previous chapters have shown that issues such as the inherent deficiencies of currency, temporal inconsistency and issues relating to the perspective scales of operations can combine to obfuscate the true significance of the data being interpreted using traditional financial performance measurement and assessment methods. The analysis of the financial performance of a business requires a measurement unit that would be free of the identified deficiencies associated with the traditional measurement units of currency, percentages and other popular methods. It was noted that the most likely solution to achieve this objective would be some form of ratio that would equate to an 'absolute' (the highest form of) measurement scale (Pike and Roos, 2007, p. 231). This chapter will introduce a technique that determines a ratio that eliminates the influence of the issues plaguing traditional techniques. This technique is one application of a technique that forms the integrated ratio analysis approach promoted in this book.

Proportional asset ratio

A number of methods that are utilised to measure the financial performance of organisations have already been examined. Although some of these techniques were found to approach the quality afforded by absolute scales, all of those methods were, unfortunately, ultimately found sufficiently wanting. It was found, for instance, that those methods could not ensure the internal and external consistency of their calculations. Furthermore, those techniques were shown to be unable to deal with the fact that individual variables within a set of financial statements are not actually autonomous of each other. This is important because for any solution to be successful, it must be able to ensure it considers the interconnectivity between all of the variables being assessed.

Although the vertical ratio technique overcame this particular aspect, even this technique is compromised by the fact that it has two different variables to form the base of the calculations it requires. It is believed that establishing a single reference point against which all calculations would be consistently made will create outputs that will possess all of the positive characteristics of existing techniques and also be free of their deficiencies. This belief is encouraged by the realisation that the very nature of the fundamental accounting equation is such that the total reported assets of any organisation would represent the *sum of the whole* of the business. This will be true regardless of the magnitude of the currency value (overcoming issues of perspective scale) and will be consistent for every year that financial statements are prepared for and for every business being assessed (overcoming issues relating to temporal consistency and internal and external comparability).

As a result, the accounting equation is perfectly suited to form the basis of an absolute measurement scale ratio for the purpose of assessing the financial performance of a business. Represented by the variable A in the accounting equation $A = L + P$, the Total Assets of a business are always defined to be the outcome of the contributions from the owners (P) and borrowed from creditors (L). Subsequently, it follows that the Total Assets variable can always be expressed in mathematical terms as 100 per cent, or 1, and all of the contributing variables some fraction thereof. If the variables that financed the resources (Total Assets) of a business are converted into fractions of that whole, a perfect measure is created of the relative impact these sources have had, in terms of their contribution to the business. This system of ratios will henceforth be called proportional asset ratios (PAR).

The concept and relationships of PAR analysis are defined by Equation 4.1. A practical illustration of the application of this method is provided in Figure 4.1. The ratio that is represented by this equation ensures that no matter how large (or small) the numerical value of Total Assets is for an organisation, *every* organisation can be directly comparable by totally eliminating the influence of perspective scale. Because this method utilises a *single* reference point (Total Assets) for all of its calculations for both financial statements (trading statement and balance sheet), it overcomes the problems that beset the vertical ratio technique. The manner in which the PAR technique achieves this for the trading statement will be examined in a later section.

Proportional asset ratio equation

The traditional accounting balance sheet equation is expressed thus:

Assets (A) = Liabilities (L) + Proprietorship (P)

Therefore, with both sides equating to each other, the balance sheet equation could be rearranged into the following (PAR) format:

$$\left(\frac{L+P}{A}\right) = 1.0 \tag{4.1}$$

The illustration of Equation 4.1 will utilise the values for balance sheet variables for AUSPA obtained from their 2010 financial statements as follows:

$$\left(\frac{\$46,884,000 + \$48,320,000}{\$95,164,000}\right) = 1.0$$

Figure 4.1 An example of the application of Equation 4.1.

Expanded PAR equation

In a similar way to the Proprietorship variable, the Liabilities class is a summary category for many forms of variables that are classified in this grouping. The Proprietorship variable, however, is fundamentally different. This is because the Proprietorship classification actually represents three major subgroupings within its purview. The first of these is Contributed Capital. This category groups together all of the variables that represent the resources contributed directly by the owners. The second category contains all of the variables that represent resources that have been generated from wealth creation from *non*-trading activities. This category is called Reserves. The final category represents the accumulated results from trading activities by an organisation over time and is called Retained Earnings.

There are many different types of Reserves that are established for a number of different reasons and from various types of sources. While some types of Reserves can be aligned closely to income streams and can, therefore, be aligned with Retained Earnings, others can be more closely aligned to Introduced Capital (belonging to the owners). In the light of the ambiguity surrounding which category Reserves are more appropriately aligned with for the purposes of PAR analysis, any type of Reserve will be classified as a separate variable. It is important, for the understanding of PAR analysis, that the different forms of contributions represented by the single proprietorship classification are separated. For this reason, the relationship defined by Equation 4.1 is expanded to include Introduced Capital $\left(\hat{C}\right)$, Retained Earnings $\left(\pi^{r}\right)$ and the level of Reserves (ϖ) that a business may have set aside. The resulting fully expanded version of the PAR can, subsequently, be described as per Equation 4.2. A worked example of this variation of the PAR equation is provided in Figure 4.2.

Amended asset funding relationship equation

The traditional accounting balance sheet equation can be expanded as follows:

$$\text{Assets}(A) = \text{Liabilities}(L) + \left[\text{Introduced Capital}\left(\hat{C}\right) \text{Retained Earnings } \left(\pi^{r}\right) \right. \\ \left. + \textit{Reserves } \left(\varpi\right) \right]$$

Therefore, with both sides equating to each other, the balance sheet equation could be rearranged thus:

$$\left(\frac{L_t + \left(\hat{C}_t + \pi_t + \varpi_t\right)}{A_t} \right) = 1.0 \tag{4.2}$$

To illustrate Equation 4.2, the values of variables for AUSPA from their 2010 published financial statements will be utilised as follows:

$$\left(\frac{\$46,844,000 + \left(\$47,992,000 + \$0 + \$328,000\right)}{\$95,164,000} \right) = 1.0$$

Figure 4.2 An example of the application of Equation 4.2.

Trading variables and the PAR concept

To this point in time, the PAR methodology is actually identical to the balance sheet portion of the vertical ratio analysis methodology. Where the PAR method differs from the vertical ratio analysis technique is that it combines the analysis of the separate financial statements into a single task. This variation is fundamentally sound, from a theoretical standpoint, because the individual trading statement variables are technically represented by the π^{r} variable of the PAR Equation 4.2. Consequently, as expressed by Equation 4.3 and illustrated in Figure 4.3, the PAR values for the individual profit and loss elements that contribute to π^{r} (such as Income (Y), Expenses (E) and Operating Profit (π)) can also be determined by dividing their values by the value of Total Assets (A).

This process will not only ensure that the results would have a greater level of internal consistency between the different financial statements, but they would also better reflect the relative earning capacity of different businesses than the use of either the vertical ratio analysis (VRA) methodology or currency values on their own.

Trading PAR relationship (Equation 4.3)

The calculation of the trading statement PAR values is applied as follows:

[Income (Y)/ Total Assets (A)] – [Expenses (E) / Total Assets (A) = [Operating Result (π^r) / Total Assets (A)]; or

$$\left[\frac{Y-E}{A}\right] = \left[\frac{\pi^r}{A}\right] \tag{4.3}$$

To illustrate Equation 4.3, the values variables for AUSPA from their 2010 financial statements reported in Table 2.9 will be calculated as follows:

$$= \left[\frac{\$58,250,000 - \$46,443,000}{\$95,164,000}\right] = \left[\frac{\$11,807,000}{\$95,164,000}\right]$$
$$= 0.612 - 0.488 = 0.124$$

Figure 4.3 An example of the application of Equation 4.3.

The PAR technique and inherent context

The ability of an analyst to instantly appreciate not only the quantity of a measurement but also the significance of that measurement without reference to any other information is what is referred to by inherent context. Any form of ratio will, generally, automatically possess this quality. In most applications, an analyst will be able to appreciate the quantity and quality of a measurement that is expressed as a ratio. In addition to being a technique that produces ratio values, the PAR methodology is able to ensure that every value for every variable for both financial statements will have the same contextual reference of the Total Assets of the business to which it has been applied. As a result, the outputs of the PAR technique will definitely possess the characteristic of inherent context.

The PAR technique and temporal consistency

Similar to the VRA methodology, the PAR technique is applied to the variables contained within the data set for one specific time period. As a result of this, the values that are determined through this technique will always be temporally consistent. Unfortunately, what this also means is that because the technique does not assess performances across periods, this method cannot be used to ascertain any trends of numerical growth (as opposed to organic/holistic growth) in the value of variables.

The PAR technique and different forms of currency

One of the benefits of the PAR method is that it ensures the comparison of businesses that report in different currencies can occur without the need to first convert the data into a common currency unit. Once currency values have been transformed into a PAR, the value will validly be comparable to any other PAR value without the need for any further conversion. This can be illustrated by converting the currency values for the 2010 financial information for the three professional bodies (AUSPA, UKPA and USPA) contained in Table 2.9 into PAR values. The outcomes of this application are summarised in Table 4.1 and enable an instant comparison of performance between these organisations.

The conversion of the numerical currency values of the information provided in Table 2.9 into PAR ratios has instantly eliminated the need to convert any of those values into a common currency unit. As a result, any changes in the exchange rates between those different currencies can be completely ignored when analysing their results if the PAR technique has been utilised. It must be emphasised, however, that any conclusions derived from the analysis in this specific exercise must be tempered by the understanding that the professional bodies in question are *not* profit-maximising ventures. Nevertheless, it can be concluded that based on the PAR values that have been calculated, AUSPA could be considered the best-performing entity of those being examined in terms of possessing the largest surplus. Despite, with a value of 0.612 in Table 4.1, generating nearly half the PAR value for Fee Income for UKPA, the PAR value for the Surplus of AUSPA (at 0.124 in Table 4.1) was at least three times larger than the PAR values for this variable for its counterparts.

Impressively, it can readily be determined that UKPA managed to generate Fee Income that was 17.6 per cent more than its entire asset base value

Table 4.1 PAR values for 2010 financial data for three professional associations[a]

Variable	USPA	UKPA	AUSPA
	A_O	A_O	A_O
Fee Income	0.478	1.176	0.612
Surplus	0.039	0.033	0.124
Total Assets	1	1	1
Total Liabilities	0.786	0.631	0.492
Total Equity	0.214	0.369	0.508

a Determined from information in Table 2.9.

(understanding that the PAR value for Total Assets is 1.000). Another conclusion that can be made from the values in Table 4.1 is that USPA has a
significantly higher proportion of Liabilities (0.786 per Table 4.1) to Equity
(0.2144 per Table 4.1) than any of its counterparts. This would normally
be of some concern when determining the future viability of an organisation. However, for this specific situation, it is important to understand that
a large amount of the Liabilities variable for these organisations represent
membership fees paid in advance. The large discrepancies between these
organisations for this variable could simply be a result of the timing of the
collection of the fees in relation to the reporting date of the balance sheet
information. This may be something the organisations such as USPA might
want to consider once armed with this knowledge.

The PAR technique and perspective scale

The selected financial information for the three professional associations
will be utilised to demonstrate the capabilities of the PAR system in relation
to the issue of perspective scale. To assist this demonstration, the currency
values (without conversion) for the financial variables for 2010 for the three
professional bodies are presented in Figure 4.4. The large disparities in the
sizes (numerically) of the Total Assets values for the three entities in this
example are apparent in Figure 4.4. This figure emphasises the impact of
perspective scale on attempts to compare the performance of different organisations. Because of the variations in the respective sizes of Total Assets,
none of the differences in the variables that are visible in Figure 4.4 can be
treated as actual dissimilarities in performance.

The impact of perspective scale on the analysis of financial performance is
demonstrated by the Fee Income variable in Figure 4.4. It is visibly apparent

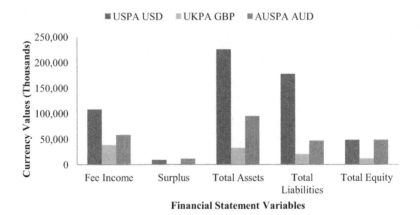

Figure 4.4 Key financial data for three professional associations for 2010[a].
a Determined from information in Table 2.9.

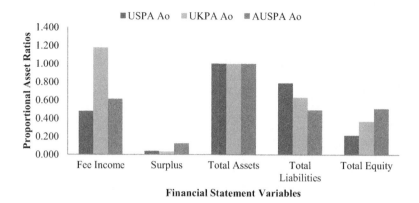

Figure 4.5 PAR values for key 2010 financial variables for three professional
associations[a].
a Determined from information in Table 4.1.

that the pattern of the columns for Fee Income is virtually identical to that
for the Total Assets in Figure 4.4. This illustrates how conclusions about
the level of performance of a financial variable cannot be made solely on
its numerical value. Fortunately, the PAR-equivalent representation of the
currency values depicted in Figure 4.5 demonstrates how the technique
'normalises' the data (with Total Assets values that equate). Once the Total
Asset values (size of the organisations) have been normalised in this manner, the effects of perspective scale is eliminated and direct comparisons of
the performance of the remaining variables can be made instantaneously.

In Figure 4.4, for example, USPA had the largest numerical value for
Membership Fees of the three organisations in the example. However, once
the impact of perspective scale has been removed through the application
of the PAR technique, the normalised values in Figure 4.5 show that USPA
actually generated the lowest proportional rate of Membership Fees. Conversely, although UKPA possessed the lowest numerical value for Membership Fee income in Figure 4.4, it actually possessed the largest normalised
value for this variable in Figure 4.5. This simple example demonstrates how
the PAR methodology is able to eliminate the influence of perspective scale
for the purpose of measuring and assessing financial performance.

The PAR technique as an absolute scale

To be regarded as an absolute measurement scale (classified as the highest
form of measurement scale), it must faithfully represent all of the characteristics of the element being measured (Pike and Roos, 2007). The PAR
technique achieves this by providing ratio values that replicate their currency-
equivalent values in a linear relationship. This is illustrated by Figure 4.6,

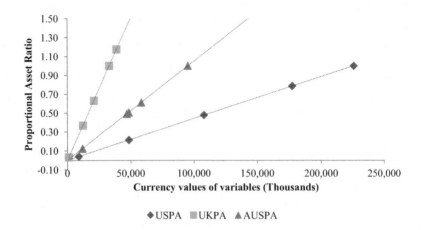

◆USPA   ◼UKPA   ▲AUSPA

Figure 4.6 PAR relationship to currency values for three professional bodies[a].
a Determined from information in Table 2.1 and Table 4.1.

which depicts the relationships between the currency values of the selected financial variables for the three professional bodies and their PAR-equivalent values. Each point in Figure 4.6 represents the intersection of a currency value and its PAR value for a specific financial variable. Lines have been added that connect these points for each organisation. The perfectly linear format of the lines indicates that the PAR technique perfectly reflects the currency values that they purport to represent. Whereas a currency value for a variable has no inherent context, a PAR value for that variable innately indicates the proportional relationship to the Total Assets of that organisation (by definition). In this way, it is understood that the larger a PAR value, the more significant to the organisation that value is. Combined with the knowledge that the linear relationships depicted in Figure 4.6 provide a great deal of confidence in their representation, any conclusions about the performance of any of the variables for the professional bodies in this example can be instantaneous and definitive.

The superior levels of comparability that the PAR methodology provides allow analysts to benchmark the performances of one specific variable of interest at a time. As an example, Figure 4.7 charts the relationship between the PAR values for the Fee Income variable for the three professional bodies (obtained from Table 4.1) to their currency values from which they were derived (obtained from Table 2.1). Not only is it clear from Figure 4.7 that UKPA possessed the best PAR result for Fee Income generated, it did so from the smallest base. Conversely, USPA generated the lowest PAR value for Fee Income from the largest currency base.

The analysis that was conducted for Fee Income can be replicated for the Surplus variable. Consequently, the PAR values for the Surplus of the three professional bodies listed in Table 4.1 were also isolated and compared to their currency-equivalent values. The results are depicted in Figure 4.8. In this example, the point in Figure 4.8 that is labelled AUSPA appears to indicate that this organisation not only generated the highest currency value surplus, but it has also achieved this with the highest PAR value. If the three organisations that are being assessed were profit-maximising ventures, then the results achieved by AUSPA would, undoubtedly, result in the conclusion that it was the stand-out performer among the bodies being reviewed.

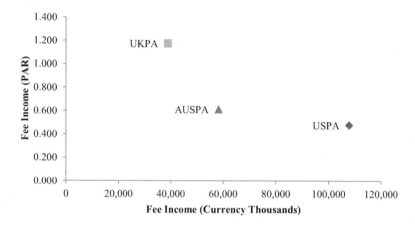

Figure 4.7 PAR and currency relationship for three professional bodies (2010 Fee Income).

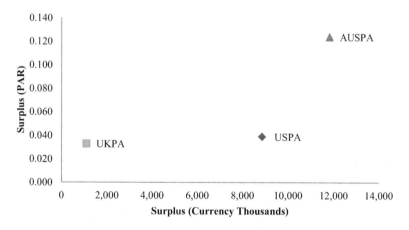

Figure 4.8 PAR and currency relationship for three professional bodies (2010 Surplus).

Case study: PAR analysis of GM financials

The financial statement values reported in GM's (General Motors')Annual Reports for the years 2009–2011 (as reported in Figure 2.1) were selected to demonstrate the intricacies of the PAR methodology. The formulae defined in Equations 4.1 to 4.3 were applied to the data reported in Figure 2.1 to create the PAR values that are contained in Figure 4.9. Unlike some of the other methods examined, because the PAR methodology is applied to

	2009 PAR	2010 PAR	2011 PAR
Trading Statement			
Revenue			
Automotive Sales	0.767	0.973	1.029
GM Financial Revenue	0	0.002	0.01
Total Revenue	0.767	0.975	1.039
Expenses			
Automotive Cost of Sales	0.823	0.855	0.902
GM Financial Expenses	0	0.001	0.005
Automotive Selling, General & Admin	0.089	0.082	0.084
Other Automotive Expenses	0.009	0.001	0
Goodwill Impairment	0	0	0.009
Total Costs & Expenses	0.921	0.939	1
Operating Income / (loss)	-0.154	0.036	0.039
Balance Sheet			
Assets			
Automotive Current Assets	0.435	0.382	0.417
Automotive Non-Current Assets	0.565	0.539	0.493
GM Financial Assets	0	0.079	0.09
Total Assets	1	1	1
Liabilities			
Automotive Current Liabilities	0.385	0.34	0.338
Automotive Non-Current Liabilities	0.403	0.34	0.331
GM Finance Liabilities	0	0.053	0.061
Total Liabilities	0.788	0.732	0.73
Net Assets	0.212	0.268	0.27
Equity	0.212	0.268	0.27
Total Equity	0.212	0.268	0.27

Figure 4.9 Proportional Asset Ratio (PAR) values for GM (2009–2011)[a].
a Determined by applying the PAR technique to data in Figure 2.1.

the information for a specific time frame, the technique is able to provide a value for any variable that has a monetary amount in the first year of analysis (2009 for this example in Figure 4.9). The second positive comparison to other techniques examined is that there are also no 'ERR' outputs resulting from a calculation made in relation to variables with a zero base value. This particular characteristic extends to situations where a base value may be negative. It is clear, for example, that the PAR values for the Operating Income/(loss) variable accurately reflect the negative or positive status of the currency values for that period as reported in Figure 2.1.

Acknowledging that the PAR method is very similar to the VRA technique, additional analysis in this section requires a direct comparison between these approaches. Most importantly, a comparison between the VRA and PAR techniques must concede that any inquiry of balance sheet variables will (in most instances) produce *identical* results and conclusions. This is because both techniques utilise the Total Asset variable (although the VRA technique could be forced to use the Total Liabilities variable in some instances) in the balance sheet as the base to determine the ratios for all other balance sheet variables. Where the PAR methodology fundamentally diverges from the VRA technique, however, is in the treatment of the information contained within the trading statement. Whereas the VAR method will utilise the variable with the largest value in the trading statement to form the base for other trading statement variables, the PAR technique will continue to use the Total Assets value. As a result of this difference, the ratios determined by the PAR technique for trading statement variables are far more meaningful and internally consistent.

Unlike what can happen for the VRA technique (refer to discussion on Figure 3.5), the consistent use of a balance sheet base variable for the trading statement variables in the PAR analysis allows insight to be generated and conclusions to be made for *all* trading variables for all periods examined. To begin with, the PAR values for Total Revenue in Figure 4.9 reveal that GM enjoyed a holistic increase from the 2009 value of 0.767 to the 2011 value of 1.039. Over the same period of time, the Total Costs and Expenses for GM only grew from 0.921 in 2009 to 1.000 in 2011 (refer to Figure 4.9). The combined increase in the size of income generated and the containment of expenses enabled the dramatic turnaround in profitability from −0.154 in 2009 to 0.039 in 2011 (refer to Figure 4.9).

Indeed, the performance of these variables resulted in the PAR value of 0.039 for the 2011 Operating Surplus. Given the quality of the PAR measure, this result can confidently be determined to be the best result for GM over the period of the analysis. This was, however, a very close outcome because the result for 2010 was, at 0.036 (refer to Figure 4.9), only just behind in quality. A review of the PAR results reported in Figure 4.9 will need to keep in mind that the values for the trading variables under the PAR method were determined in a very different basis. For example, while the value of GM's Financial Revenue for 2010 was 21 per cent of Total Revenue (refer to Figure 4.9), the PAR value for 2010 was 0.002 of Total Assets (refer to Figure 4.9). The value for the PAR calculation for this variable suggests that, for the year 2010, this variable was very insignificant to the overall operations of GM.

Although an increase in the PAR value of this variable to 0.10 of the Total Assets in 2011 (refer to Figure 4.9) confirms that the actual growth *for that variable* was significant, the importance of this variable to the overall operations of GM was, nevertheless, not significant. This would support the reasoning behind the omission in the statements from the Chairman and CEO of any discussion around the growth in this particular variable. This form of analysis can, of course, be replicated for the expenses that relate to the GM Financial operations conducted by GM. Rather than comparing the PAR results to those from other techniques, however, this analysis will be brief and focus only on the results from the PAR analysis for this variable. The PAR values for the GM Financial Expenses variable were 0.001 for 2010 and 0.005 for 2011 (refer to Figure 4.9). These were, again, relatively insignificant for the overall operations of GM for those years. Having said that, the overall gross profitability of the GM Financial operations for those years, at 50 per cent, appears to have been substantial for that variable.

PAR analysis of GM financial operations segment and comparison to other techniques

The utility of the PAR technique can be emphasised by the simple analysis of one segment of the operations of GM in this period. The segment selected for analysis is the GM Financial operations. The 2011 Annual Report for GM stated that this segment of their operations '...specializes in purchasing retail automobile instalment sales contracts originated by GM and non-GM franchised and select independent dealers in connection with the sale of used and new automobiles' (2011 GM Annual Report, p. 211). A simple review of the financial information in Figure 4.9 indicates that although this segment was not operating in 2009 and represents only a small fraction of the total business activity for GM, it seems that this part of their business was not only growing rapidly, but also appeared to be very profitable. Intriguingly, despite this apparently significant rate of growth and positive level of profitability for this segment, there is nothing mentioned of this aspect of the operations of GM in the report of the Chairman and CEO of the company presented in the 2011 Annual Report.

If an assessment of the performance of the GM Financial Revenue variable were to be made on the changes in currency values alone, it would be reasonable to conclude that an average growth of $0.705 billion per annum was a reasonably impressive result (refer to Figure 2.2). Despite the fact that this would represent an enormous amount of money for *many* other businesses, in terms of the specific analysis for GM, however, the income from this part of their operations did not even account for 1 per cent of their total reported revenue in 2011. Quite clearly, it would be desirable to have some other measure that could be utilised to ascertain the significance of the performance of this part of the GM operations.

With no reported currency value for the GM Financial Revenue variable for 2009 (refer to Figure 2.1), the percentage change (refer to Figure 3.1) and anchored horizontal ratio analysis (refer to Figure 3.4) methodologies are incapable of providing any values for the 2010 financial year for this variable. For the 2011 financial year, the percentage change method provided a value of 401.78 per cent (refer to Figure 3.1), the anchored horizontal ratio method provided an error (Err) value (refer to Figure 3.4) and the vertical ratio method provided a value of 0.94 (refer to Figure 3.5).

It is acknowledged that the 2011 numerical increase in the GM Financial Revenue from the 2009 base was a significant currency value (refer to Figure 2.2). It is also accepted that the calculation of 401.78 per cent for the change itself is mathematically sound (refer to Figure 3.1). Based on this information, it would appear (on a prima-facie basis) that the performance of this variable was significant for this business. The results from other techniques, however, would suggest otherwise. If, for example, the vertical ratio technique were utilised instead, the result of 0.94 for 2011 for this variable (refer to Figure 3.5) indicates that the significance of this segment for GM may not have been as important as the percentage change and currency techniques suggest. Although the reported vertical ratio value of 0.94 for the year 2011 still represents an increase of around 347 per cent of the vertical ratio value of 0.21 in 2010, the level of *significance* of this increase is better reflected by the ratio than by the percentage change approach.

To further confuse matters, if the anchored version of the horizontal ratio analysis approach were adopted for this analysis, there would actually be no values at all that would be determinable for this segment for GM because there was no base value available in 2009 (refer to Figure 3.4). Fortunately, the use of the PAR method is able to not only quantify the level of performance for this variable, but also qualify the value of the performance of this variable to the organisation. The PAR value for the GM Financial Revenue variable for 2011 was only 0.010 (refer to Figure 4.9). This demonstrates that while the currency value of this variable for this segment may have generated a significant level of growth, its value to the organisation as a whole was almost negligible. This would account for the fact that this segment was deemed not of sufficient value for mention in the Annual Report by the most senior management of the organisation.

Case study: proportional asset ratios for Australian banks

This case study seeks to utilise the PAR method to analyse the financial performance of four Australian banks. The selection of Australian banking institutions was based on the notion that this industry has been so heavily regulated by government in Australia, there would be little comparative variation between them and would, consequently, be an ideal choice to demonstrate the capabilities of the PAR methodology. Historically, there have been four banks that have shared the majority of the market in the Australian banking sector, '...accounting for almost 80 per cent of resident assets' (IMF Country Report No 12/311, 2012, p. 5). Given that they were of a similar size (in terms of their relative systemic performance – IMF Country Report No 12/311, 2012, p. 8), three of these four banks were selected for use in this illustration.

On this basis, the institutions chosen for this illustration were the Commonwealth Bank of Australia (CBA), National Australia Bank (NAB) and Westpac Banking Corporation (WBC). The ANZ Bank was excluded from this exercise because it was the smallest of the four major banks in terms of their market share and Total Assets. The Bank of Queensland (BOQ) was also selected for comparison in this exercise in order to illustrate the effects and influence of perspective scale (being the last bank in Table 3 of IMF Country Report No 12/311, 2012, p. 8 supports this selection) as illustrated in Chapter 1.

The information for this case study will commence with the currency values for the main financial variables from their financial statements for the 2006 financial year as presented in Table 4.2. Although this information may appear to be dated at the time of this publication, it was felt that there was no real need to update the information for this specific case study. This example was heavily relied upon in the development of the integrated ratio analysis methodology and has been reproduced herein to illustrate the finer analytical ability of this technique. The fact that this data is not entirely current does not affect the impact of its use to illustrate the techniques that are being expounded herein. The application of the PAR methodology as prescribed by Equations 4.1–4.3 to the currency values contained in Table 4.2 will result in the PAR values as summarised in Table 4.3.

It is apparent from the information in Table 4.2 that, in terms of the currency values of the reported Total Assets figures, BOQ is a considerably smaller enterprise in comparison to the other three nominated institutions. Unfortunately, other than possibly indicating the relative differences in size between the four banks, the data provided in the format presented in Table 4.2 provides little in the way of additional understanding of the comparative financial performance of these banks. The converted PAR values contained in Table 4.3, however, provide reliable insights into their comparative capital structures and performances that can be readily and simply determined. Although, for example, Table 4.2 shows that, in terms of numerical currency values, WBC (with Total Assets of AU\$ 299.58 billion) is around 19 times the size of BOQ (with Total Assets of AU\$ 15.80 billion), the PAR values contained in Table 4.3 indicate that, in *relative* terms, they are financed in very similar proportions (with Liability PAR ratios that are very close in value).

The information contained in Table 4.3 also indicates that despite earning the least amount of income in currency terms (AU\$ 1.132 billion in Table 4.2), BOQ actually managed to generate a similar ratio of Income to Total Assets (0.0717) as WBC (0.0723). It can also be observed that despite NAB and CBA having *identical* Liabilities to Asset ratios (at 0.9423), they

Table 4.2 Financial data of four Australian banks for 2006 financial year

Variable	CBA	NAB	WBC	BOQ
	AUD (M)	AUD (M)	AUD (M)	AUD (M)
Total Income	28,564	38,235	21,666	1,132
Operating Profit	12,286	15,523	9,217	385
Total Assets	3,69,103	4,84,785	2,99,578	15,797
Total Liabilities	3,47,760	4,56,813	2,83,480	15,107
Introduced Capital	14,952	12,447	7,380	531
Retained Earnings	4,487	14,461	8,532	98
Reserves	1,904	1,064	186	61

Obtained from 2006 Annual Reports (various).

Table 4.3 Proportional Asset Ratios of four Australian banks for 2006 financial year

Variable	CBA	NAB	WBC	BOQ
	A_0	A_0	A_0	A_0
Income	0.0774	0.0789	0.0723	0.0717
Operating Profit	0.0333	0.032	0.0308	0.0244
Assets	1	1	1	1
Liabilities	0.9423	0.9423	0.9463	0.9563
Introduced Capital	0.0405	0.0257	0.0246	0.0336
Retained Earnings	0.012	0.0298	0.0285	0.0062
Reserves	0.0052	0.0022	0.0006	0.0039

A_0 = Proportional Asset Ratios for 2006 financial year. Calculated from Table 4.2.

differ in their Introduced Capital ratios. The Introduced Capital PAR for CBA of 0.0405 was significantly (in PAR terms) higher than the PAR of 0.0257 for NAB (refer to Table 4.3). The difference in the financing structures of CBA and NAB has an important impact on their relative financial performance. NAB performed better, in terms of generating revenue, with a PAR of 0.0789 for Income that is compared to a PAR of 0.0774 for CBA (refer to Table 4.3). CBA, however, was able to manage a PAR of 0.0333 for their Operating Profit, which was not only better than the 0.0320 for NAB, but also the highest of all four banks (refer to Table 4.3). Despite this, the greater reliance on their Introduced Capital than NAB has meant that CBA had a lower Return on Capital than NAB.

The Return on Capital is determined by dividing the Operating Profit PAR value by the Introduced Capital PAR value. Using the values in Table 4.3, the Return on Capital ratio of 0.82 for CBA (Operating Profit PAR of 0.0333 divided by Introduced Capital PAR of 0.0405 per Table 4.3) was much lower than the ratio of 1.25 for NAB (Operating Profit PAR of 0.0320 divided by Introduced Capital PAR of 0.0257 per Table 4.3). Noting that it required up to four decimal places in order to distinguish the differences in some of the variables for the businesses selected for comparison, the ratio outcomes listed in Table 4.3 indicate that the selection of these institutions and industry was ideal for the purposes of illustrating the value of the PAR methodology. Indeed, even though the PAR values in Table 4.3 are presented to *four* decimal places, it demonstrates that CBA and NAB had *identical* Liability PAR values.

Certainly not in any way, and nor was it meant to be, a complete analysis of the information presented in Table 4.3, any conclusions derived from an examination of this nature can, nevertheless, be made with confidence. This is because of the ability of the PAR technique to ensure that all of the information relating to financial performance is presented on a level-playing field. One of the key features of an absolute scale is that it completely represents the attribute that it is purported to measure. It should, subsequently, provide great comfort to any user of the PAR methodology that this is a characteristic that is certainly possessed by the technique.

This claim can be substantiated with the recognition that when the currency value of the financial variables being analysed are directly compared to their equivalent PAR calculation, the resulting relationship is perfectly linear. This is confirmed by comparing the PAR values in Table 4.3 in direct relationship to their currency values in Table 4.2 as demonstrated by Figure 4.10. This figure demonstrates that there is a linear relationship for each bank selected in this case study in *every* instance examined. A linear relationship is a significant finding because it allows the *direct* comparison of the financial variables for businesses through the use of PAR scales with the complete elimination of issues relating to perspective scale and currency translations with total confidence in the validity of the comparison.

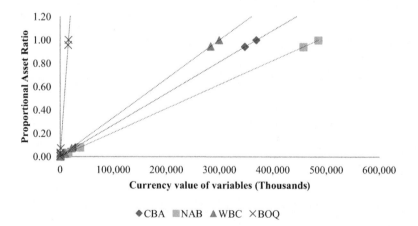

◆CBA ■NAB ▲WBC ✕BOQ

Figure 4.10 Proportional Asset Ratios and currency values for four Australian banks for 2006[a].
a Determined from information in Tables 4.2 and 4.3.

Extension of the proportional asset ratio analysis for banking case study

With the issue of perspective scale genuinely neutralised by the PAR methodology, the comparison of financial variables becomes more meaningful. The PAR methodology allows an instant assessment as to which organisation performed the best for any specific variable and by precisely what extent for any particular period of time. In addition to providing improved comparability between businesses, the PAR methodology (through changes in PAR values over time) also enables the assessment of whether variable changes are merely numeric (in proportion to changes in the size of the actual business) or organic (changes are actually reflective of the performance of that variable irrespective of changes to the size of the business). This ability can be demonstrated through an extension of the PAR analysis of the banking case study. To aid this illustration, the values for the 2007 financial year for the variables in Table 4.2 were obtained. The currency values for these variables are summarised in Table 4.4, and the converted PAR values are presented in Table 4.5. The currency changes between the 2007 currency values from the 2006 values have been determined and are presented in Table 4.6. The PAR values for these currency changes are illustrated in Table 4.7.

The currency changes between the values in Tables 4.2 and 4.4 and reported in Table 4.6 show that the numerical currency values for all variables in the data set have increased. Despite this, and although they are reported in the same currency unit, the figures reported in Table 4.6 cannot, individually, or in comparison to each other, provide any qualitative insight for the results of any variable for any bank. For example, although a positive increase in Total Income of AU$ 6,213 million for NAB (refer to Table 4.6) is 'good' (in comparison to any result less than that), it cannot be deduced from this information *how* good the result was. Similarly, just because this value is also the largest increase of this variable of the four banks examined in Table 4.6, it cannot automatically be deduced that this result was the *best* of the four reported

Table 4.4 Financial data of four Australian banks for 2007 financial year

Variable	CBA	NAB	WBC	BOQ
	AUD (M)	AUD (M)	AUD (M)	AUD (M)
Total Income	33,169	44,448	25,935	1,490
Operating Profit	13,391	16,029	10,173	500
Total Assets	4,25,139	5,64,634	3,74,821	20,037
Total Liabilities	4,00,695	5,34,749	3,49,286	19,183
Introduced Capital	15,422	12,755	7,923	616
Retained Earnings	6,367	16,059	9,716	151
Reserves	2,143	1,071	192	88

Obtained from 2007 Annual Reports (various).

Table 4.5 Proportional Asset Ratios of four Australian banks for 2007 financial year

Variable	CBA	NAB	WBC	BOQ
	A_0	A_0	A_0	A_0
Income	0.078	0.0787	0.0692	0.0744
Operating Profit	0.0315	0.0284	0.0271	0.025
Assets	1	1	1	1
Liabilities	0.9425	0.9471	0.9319	0.9574
Introduced Capital	0.0363	0.0226	0.0211	0.0307
Retained Earnings	0.015	0.0284	0.0259	0.0075
Reserves	0.005	0.0019	0.0005	0.0044

A_0 = Proportional asset ratios for 2007 financial year. Calculated from Table 4.4.

Table 4.6 Currency changes in variables for four Australian banks from 2006 to 2007

Variable	CBA	NAB	WBC	BOQ
	(Δ AUS million)	(Δ AUS million)	(Δ AUS million)	(Δ AUS million)
Income	4,605	6,213	4,269	358
Operating Profit	1,105	506	956	115
Assets	56,036	79,849	75,243	4,240
Liabilities	52,935	77,936	65,806	4,076
Introduced Capital	470	308	543	85
Retained Earnings	1,880	1,598	1,184	53
Reserves	239	7	6	27

Calculated by deducting 2006 currency values (Table 4.2) from 2007 currency values (Table 4.4).

Table 4.7 PAR changes of four Australian banks for 2007 financial year from 2006

Variable	CBA	NAB	WBC	BOQ
	ΔA_0	ΔA_0	ΔA_0	ΔA_0
Income	0.0006	−0.0002	−0.0031	0.0027
Operating Profit	−0.0018	−0.0036	−0.0037	0.0006
Assets	0	0	0	0
Liabilities	0.0002	0.0048	−0.0144	0.0011
Introduced Capital	−0.0042	−0.0031	−0.0035	−0.0029
Retained Earnings	0.003	−0.0014	−0.0026	0.0013
Reserves	−0.0002	−0.0003	−0.0001	0.0005

A_0 = Calculated by deducting 2006 PAR values (Table 4.3) from 2007 PAR values (Table 4.5).

values. It appears, therefore, that while the currency-based interval technique provides a modicum of additional utility over simple currency values, it is not sufficient to impart qualitative insight into financial performance.

The inability to form (valid) conclusions about the quality of financial performance is an issue that arises because of the phenomenon of perspective scale (particularly between different organisations). This shortcoming extends to the currency-based interval technique, which, consequently, will not be much more enlightening when applied *within* the same organisation either. An example of this is that, while the currency-based interval increases of AU\$ 358 million in Total Income and AU\$ 115 million in Operating Profit (refer to Table 4.6) for BOQ provides analysts with the *quantum* of change in variable values, they do not provide the *qualitative* insight into the changes that is actually required. Unlike the currency values, however, the PAR values enable an instant insight into the performance of the variable provided by the inherent context and elimination of the effects of perspective scale by the technique. For example, although BOQ possessed the lowest 2007 PAR value for its Operating Profit (0.0250, see Table 4.5) of all four banks (and therefore worst result for that period), it was the only bank in the group that *increased* the PAR value from its 2006 result. While the other three banks all had negative changes to their Operating Profit PAR values, the BOQ improved its Operating Profit PAR value by 0.0006 (refer to Table 4.7). As such, although the PAR for the Operating Profit of BOQ remained the lowest of the sample at the end of 2007, it can be deduced that it was the only business that improved its relative position from the previous period and was, consequently, the superior performer.

Indeed, Table 4.7 clearly illustrates that, of the four banks examined, BOQ was the *only* bank examined that demonstrated *genuine* (organic) trading-based improvements over the time frame of analysis. Given that banks generate the majority of their assets from their Liabilities, this conclusion is supported by the knowledge that BOQ reported the largest improvement in their Income (0.0027 from Table 4.7) from the lowest increase in their Liabilities (0.0011 from Table 4.7). The extent to which BOQ surpassed its competitors' results over the period of analysis (in real terms) is further emphasised by their reported improvements for Operating Profit (0.0006), Retained Earnings (0.0005) and Reserves (0.0005) in comparison to those of the other banks (refer to Table 4.7). Overall, the PAR analysis in this case study demonstrates the advantages that this technique possesses over the other financial performance analysis techniques that have been examined to date. These benefits exist because the PAR is the only technique that has inherent context, temporal consistency, is immune to currency changes and overcomes the effects of perspective scale.

Assessment of the PAR methodology

The choice of the Total Assets variable to form the singular and consistent variable for the anchoring of all of the other variables in trading statements has resulted in the PAR technique overcoming most of the issues that hampered the vertical ratio methodology. In addition, the PAR technique overcomes the negative issues relating to currency as a measurement unit. In particular, the method addresses the concerns relating to fluctuating translation rates and temporal consistency. An additional advantage of the PAR methodology over other techniques is the fact that these calculations can be performed for every variable for every period on an individual basis. As a result, the PAR technique does not succumb to the awkward situation of missing first period calculations that some other methods examined experience. This inability of some techniques renders them unable to assist the analysis of base-period financial performance.

The issue of perspective scale was found to be an important consideration in cases where direct comparisons of variable values are being made over periods of time for an individual business. This becomes a critical factor when judgements are being made in terms of the comparative performance assessment between different entities. The fact that the PAR methodology reliably provides a measure that overcomes comparability issues arising from perspective scale is, perhaps, the most significant benefit of the PAR methodology. Despite the ability of the PAR methodology to overcome issues of perspective scale for most instances, the nature of the technique results in a shortcoming of its own. Although the PAR methodology eliminates most perspective-scale issues, it also means that when it is used in isolation of other information, it is incapable of reflecting any changes over time in the sizes of variables being assessed from the outputs of that system.

Summary

In an advancement from the VRA methodology, the PAR technique proposes the use of a single variable in the balance sheet (Total Assets) to form the base for ratio calculations of all of the variables in both financial statements. This was shown to overcome the problems encountered by the VRA method that arise from selecting a variable each for the balance sheet and trading statement to enable calculations. This chapter also demonstrated how the PAR technique overcomes other issues raised in Chapter 1, such as perspective scale, currency translation, context and temporal consistency. In short, this technique meets all of the characteristics of an absolute measurement scale for financial performance measurement, analysis and benchmarking.

References

AUSPA, 2010. CPA Australia Annual Report 2010.
BOQ, 2006. BOQ Bank of Queensland Annual Report 2006.
CBA, 2006. Commonwealth Bank of Australia Annual Report 2006.
GM, 2009. GM Annual Report 2009.

GM, 2010. GM Annual Report 2010.

GM, 2011. GM Annual Report 2011.

International Monetary Fund (IMF), 2012. *Australia: Addressing Systemic Risk through Higher Loss Absorbency – Technical Note.* IMF Country Report No 12/311, IMF, Washington DC.

NAB, 2006. NAB National Australia Bank Annual Financial Report 2006.

Pike, S. and Roos, G., 2007. The Validity of Measurement Frameworks. In: A. Neely, ed. *Business Performance Measurement: Unifying Theories and Integrating Practices.* Cambridge: Cambridge University Press, pp. 218–237.

UKPA, 2010. CIMA Chartered Institute of Management Accountants, Financial Statements 2010.

USPA, 2010. AICPA American Institute of CPAs, Annual Report 2010.

WBC, 2006. Westpac Annual Financial Report 2006.

5 The anchored ratio

Abstract

It was shown in Chapter 4 that currency values for financial variables could be converted into meaningful ratios, by deriving proportional values for them against the Total Asset variable value for each period. This chapter advanced on the development of the proportional asset ratio (PAR) method with the development of the anchored ratio (AR) methodology. This involved anchoring the conversion of currency values for financial variables to the Total Assets value of a base period of analysis. This chapter also illustrated the additional benefits that were available from this difference from the PAR technique. These benefits included the ability to derive values for the Total Assets variable over time, and also the fact that the resulting ratios for all of the variables matched the patterns of growth for those variables over time. There were no major criticisms identified for this technique at this time.

Introduction

The previous chapter identified that of the techniques examined to this point, the proportional asset ratio (PAR) technique most achieved the objective of possessing all of the characteristics of an absolute measurement scale. The PAR method has a very similar application to that of the vertical ratio analysis technique. That is, it establishes a relationship for all of the financial variables within a set of financial statements for one specific period of time. It is the aim of this chapter to illustrate how the application of the PAR technique can be expanded such that it also *simultaneously* absorbs the advantages of the anchored horizontal analysis approach. This application of the PAR technique will simply be referred to as the anchored ratio (AR), and subsequently, this chapter will define, assess and demonstrate the application of the AR approach to financial performance measurement and analysis.

The impact of the growth in variable values

The PAR methodology was developed to overcome the inability of currency values to cope with comparisons involving large variations in perspective scale. Indeed, the discussion of the PAR technique showed how it was possible for two businesses that possessed significantly different perspective sizes (as measured by currency units) to have *proportionately* similar funding mixes. This is because the PAR scale reflects relative portions of a total pool and, consequently, can provide important context to any changes to the funding mix of businesses. Unfortunately, as the sum of the individual portions will always sum to the whole in the PAR equation, PAR analysis is not able to measure any changes in the *size* of the variables being examined over time and, therefore, does not facilitate the measurement of growth. For example, although Liabilities could be the same ratio of 50 per cent of Total Assets for two different years, the actual currency value of the Total Assets (and therefore size) that this ratio was assessed against could be vastly different.

This will not affect performance assessments for a single period of time (or organic growth for that matter), but it may be important for the purposes of temporal analysis. An inability to easily determine any temporal changes in the size of financial variables that are being examined may incorrectly influence any conclusions drawn in relation to the magnitude or quality of the performance being reviewed. Although one of the advantages of currency as a measurement unit is that it possesses the ability to convey changes in the size of particular variables over time for a *specific* business, it was, however, shown that this ability does not extend to the relative comparison of the changes in growth of specific variables between different businesses. What is needed, therefore, is a technique that simultaneously possesses all of the benefits of other techniques without any of their associated drawbacks.

The development of anchored ratio analysis

It is fortunate that a simple modification to the application of the PAR technique can ensure that this technique will enable an assessment of growth in the values of the variable over time. This can be achieved while simultaneously normalising the currency values into ratio values. The solution is to *anchor* the value of *every* variable to be examined, for *every* period of analysis, to the Total Assets variable of a *base* period of analysis *regardless* of the actual period that the variable value belongs to. Consequently, the outputs of this methodology can all be referred to as anchored ratios (ARs). An anchored ratio can, therefore, be defined as the ratio output created by dividing the currency value of any financial statement variable to the Total Assets currency value for a base period of analysis. Significantly, in this method of analysis, the base period does *not* have to be the very first period of trading. The Total Assets value of any period can be selected as the base period value, and this technique can be applied forwards and backwards from that point. There may be, for example, instances where care may need to be taken in the selection of the base period to ensure that it did not overly, or perversely, influence the outcome simply because the period selected was subject to extraordinary circumstances.

The fundamental notion that underlies this approach can be illustrated with the examination of how this technique would operate when applied to the Total Assets variable itself. Utilising the principles that underpin the application of the AR methodology, the calculation of the AR for the Total Assets variable would be performed in accordance with the relationship defined by Equation 5.1. This is, in turn, illustrated by an example in Figure 5.1. The resulting ratio will represent the relative size of the Total Assets variable for any period that the analysis is being conducted in direct comparison to the Total Assets variable from the period selected to form the base of the comparative analysis.

Anchored ratio equation 5.1

The AR is *almost* exactly the same as that defined by the PAR equation. The main difference between the two techniques is that all of the variables for every period, other than the base, are *anchored* to the Total Assets of a base period. Therefore, the AR (β) will be determined by dividing the Total Assets of a period of analysis (A_t) by the Total Assets of a base period of analysis (A_0). This relationship is defined as follows:

$$\beta = \left(\frac{A_t}{A_0} \right) \tag{5.1}$$

For the purposes of illustrating Equation 5.1, the values for Total Assets for AUSPA from their 2010 Annual Reports will be assigned to the variables A_0 ($84,501,000 for 2009) and A_t ($95,164,000 for 2010) as follows:

$$\beta = \left(\frac{\$95,164,000}{\$84,501,000} \right) = 1.126$$

Figure 5.1 An example of the application of Equation 5.1.

The extended development of anchored ratio analysis
for the balance sheet

It is expected that an AR will not only have the capacity to overcome the difficulties in comparing organisations that dramatically differ in perspective scale, but will also concurrently enable the calculation of growth and more meaningful comparisons of changes in growth between such entities. The application of the AR methodology is not meant to cease with comparisons between Total Asset values of different periods. Indeed, this process can be applied to *all* of the variables that represent the funding mix of the Total Asset resources in an assessed period (t). The variables that contribute the resources that represent the Total Assets of a business are, of course, the Liabilities (L) and Proprietorship (P) categories. Of these categories, the Proprietorship variable possesses additional interest. It not only represents the Introduced Capital $\left(\hat{C}\right)$ that was provided by the owners of a business, but also combines the sum contribution over time from trading $\left(\pi^r\right)$ and any Reserves (ϖ) that have been set aside or created.

AR defined by Equation 5.1 can, therefore, be expanded to indicate this expanded relationship. The expanded balance sheet version of the AR equation is, consequently, defined and illustrated by Equation 5.2. It should be noted that this equation will represent a similar calculation to that defined for the PAR methodology – albeit, in this case, the calculations are always *anchored* to the Total Assets of a base period (A_0) instead of the Total Assets for each period of analysis (A_t). A practical illustration of the expanded AR is provided in Figure 5.2.

Expanded anchored ratio equation

$$\beta = \left(\frac{L_t + \left(\hat{C}_t + \pi_t + \varpi_t\right)}{A_0}\right) = 1.0 \tag{5.2}$$

For the purposes of illustrating the calculation expressed by Equation 5.2, the values for the relevant balance sheet variables were selected for the professional organisation AUSPA from their published Annual Reports for 2010 as appropriate (refer to Table 2.9). Apart from the Total Assets variable (A_o), which was reported in 2009, all of the other values were obtained for the 2010 financial year. The calculation per Equation 5.2 for this example is determined as follows:

$$\left(\frac{\$46,844,000 + (\$47,992,000 + \$0 + \$328,000)}{\$84,501,000}\right) = 1.126$$

Or:

$$= 0.554 + (0.568 + 0.000 + 0.004) = 1.126$$

Figure 5.2 An example of the application of Equation 5.2.

Determining anchored ratios for trading statement variables

The previous section examined how the AR technique could be applied to all of the variables of a balance sheet. The expansion of the Proprietorship variable in this analysis was of particular significance. This is because this variable contained the sum result of trading over time (Retained Earnings, or π^r). In essence, this variable represents the interactions over time of all of the variables from the trading statement. This is the logical argument for why all of the trading statement variables can be treated in the same way as other balance sheet variables for this methodology. This is also the major departure from the vertical ratio analysis methodology.

   Understanding that there is a logical argument for why the trading statement can be treated in a consistent manner to that for the balance sheet variables, the AR technique could be applied to *all* of the variables of all of the financial statements in any particular assessment period (t). Although this is similar to the application of the PAR methodology, the major difference between the techniques is that every calculation is *always* anchored to the Total Assets value of a *base* period (A_0). This application will be applied in this manner even if the current period *is* the base period of analysis. The application of the AR methodology to trading statement variables is defined by Equation 5.3. A worked example of the anchored trading ratio equation 5.3 is provided in Figure 5.3. It should be noted that, as for the balance sheet variables utilised in Equation 5.2, the categories defined in Equation 5.3 represent the main headings for each type of variable and can also be expanded further.

Anchored trading ratio equation 5.3

The AR treatment of the trading statement variables is almost identical to the treatment employed by PAR technique in Equation 4.3. The only difference is that the base Total Assets value (A_0) remains the *same* for all future (or prior) periods of analysis. The application of the AR technique can be defined as follows:

$$\left[\left(\frac{\text{Income } (Y_t) - \text{Expenses } (E_t)}{\text{Total Assets } (A_o)} \right) = \left(\frac{\text{Operating Result } (\pi^r{}_t)}{\text{Total Assets } (A_o)} \right) \right] \qquad (5.3)$$

For the purposes of illustrating the calculation expressed by Equation 5.3, the values for the trading statement variables were selected for AUSPA from their published Annual Reports for 2010 as appropriate (refer to Table 2.9). Apart from the Total Assets variable (A_o), which was reported in the 2009 financial year, all of the other values were obtained from the 2010 financial year. The calculation per Equation 5.3 for this example is as follows:

$$= \left[\frac{\$58,250,000 - \$46,443,000}{\$84,501,000} \right] = \left[\frac{\$11,807,000}{\$84,501,000} \right]$$
$$= 0.689 - 0.550 = 0.139$$

Figure 5.3 An example of the application of Equation 5.3.

Anchored ratio analysis and inherent context

The outputs of the AR technique are all ratio values. Because a ratio output will always represent the relationship between more than one variable, these values will always possess an inherent context. Any user of this information will be able to appreciate the significance of the value they are studying without any reference to other extraneous information. In the same way as the PAR method is able to achieve this, the AR methodology is able to ensure that every value for every variable for both financial statements will have the same contextual reference of the Total Assets of the business to which it has been applied. The AR technique is able to extend this ability over time such that it is also able to provide an inherent context for the Total Assets variable itself. As a result, the outputs of the AR technique will definitely possess the characteristic of inherent context, and it is the only technique examined that is able to achieve this for every variable that is examined.

Anchored ratio analysis and temporal consistency

One of the key features of a quality measurement scale is that it should be temporally consistent. One of the key advantages of the AR methodology over other techniques is that the outputs of the method faithfully replicate the patterns of growth over time that the currency values of the variables being examined exhibit. As a result of this characteristic, the outputs of the AR methodology will also be temporally consistent in their reporting of the performance of the financial variables being assessed. The capabilities of the AR methodology in terms of temporal consistency can be illustrated by applying the broad concept of the technique to the hypothetical profit sequence that was initially reported in Table 4.6. It must be recognised that, for this example, there is an absence of any Total Asset values to enable the correct application of the AR in its natural use. Nevertheless, the application of the AR technique to this variable will suffice to demonstrate the ability of this method to reliably determine the growth in variables over time in a temporally consistent manner.

The values for the hypothetical profit and their representative AR values as reported in Table 5.1 have been depicted in Figure 5.4. It is clear from this representation in Figure 5.4 that the graphical depiction of the AR values in Table 5.1 perfectly reflects the growth pattern of the Hypothetical Profit in Table 5.1 over the time frame of the example. It should be noted that this is the only technique examined to date that is able to achieve this feat. This characteristic ensures that the outputs of the AR methodology have a linear relationship to the currency values from which they are derived. Furthermore, because of this ability, the use of the AR technique will result in ratio values that would be temporally consistent for both short and long time frames.

The periodical changes in the AR values contained in Table 5.1 are regular increases of 0.10 in the AR calculation. This is a direct reflection of the ten

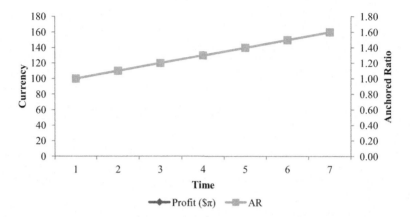

Figure 5.4 Hypothetical profit sequence and anchored ratios from Table 5.1 over time.

Table 5.1 Hypothetical profit sequence and anchored ratios

Time (t)	1	2	3	4	5	6	7
Profit (π)	100	110	120	130	140	150	160
AR	1	1.1	1.2	1.3	1.4	1.5	1.6

currency units per period increases that the Hypothetical Profit in Table 5.1 was demonstrating. If the change in the AR value for the last period in the example is compared to the AR value for the first period, the change will again directly reflect the change in the currency values from which they were derived. Even if the long-term comparison was averaged over time, the results would again perfectly align. This is an excellent illustration of how and why the AR technique is able to maintain temporal consistency. This simple demonstration illustrates how the AR methodology is the only method of those assessed in this book that has the ability to both completely mirror the growth patterns of the currency values it represents while simultaneously be temporally consistent for all variables. In other words, the AR methodology is a perfect *absolute* scale for the purpose of measuring the financial performance of a business.

The anchored ratio methodology and different currencies

One of the main benefits from the use of the AR technique is that it will allow for a direct comparison of the performance of businesses without the need for foreign currency translation. The nature of AR values will mean that once values have been converted into a ratio, the AR value will validly be directly comparable to any other AR value without the need for any further conversion. It is accepted that this is a fundamental benefit of any ratio technique. However, the knowledge that the AR method enables every single variable within a common data set to be comparable to any other variable for any other business ensures that this is a superior method to any other existing ratio. As such, this is a valuable method for the comparison of businesses that operate in different economies at times when currency translations are dramatically fluctuating.

In order to illustrate the application of the AR method to situations involving different currencies, the information for the three professional bodies used in previous chapters will, once again, be employed. Consequently, the currency values for the variables reported in Table 2.9 for the 2009 and 2010 financial years of trading for three professional bodies were used to form the basis of this example. The 2009 Total Asset values for each organisation in Table 2.9 were selected to form the base of the anchored calculations. The resulting AR values (that are reported in Table 5.2) have eliminated the need for any currency conversion and, therefore, unlike the currency values reported in Table 2.9, the AR values in Table 5.2 are totally comparable for each variable being analysed.

Although the PAR technique also achieves these outcomes, it remains unable to provide any insight into the Total Assets variable. This is because the Total Assets value for each period of analysis is used as a base for the PAR technique for that period and, accordingly, will never reflect any change in growth. This is where the supremacy of the AR technique truly comes to the fore. It is noted that the Total Assets value for each of the three bodies in the 2009 financial year in Table 5.2 is 1.0. While this result (and all other values for 2009) is exactly the same as would be generated by the PAR technique, the values for the Total Assets variable for each of the organisations in 2010, however, have changed. The AR values for 2010 for all of the remaining variables for all of the organisations will also be different from those determined by the PAR method.

Table 5.2 AR values of key financial data for three professional associations[a]

Variable	USPA		UKPA		AUSPA	
	2009	*2010*	*2009*	*2010*	*2009*	*2010*
	AR	*AR*	*AR*	*AR*	*AR*	*AR*
Membership Fees	0.448	0.465	1.166	1.217	0.647	0.689
Surplus	−0.018	0.038	0.029	0.034	0.042	0.14
Total Assets	1	0.972	1	1.034	1	1.126
Total Liabilities	0.87	0.764	0.669	0.653	0.565	0.554
Total Equity	0.13	0.208	0.331	0.381	0.435	0.572

a Determined from the currency values reported in Table 2.9.

A review of the results in Table 5.2 reveals that the Total Assets of USPA contracted in size from 1.0000 to 0.972. Despite this, the Membership Fees income for USPA actually rose from 0.448 to 0.465 (refer to Table 5.2). Interestingly, despite the currency values for the Membership Fees of UKPA being the lowest numerically of the three bodies (refer to Table 2.9), it demonstrated a far superior performance of generating revenue than the other two bodies. The AR ratios of 1.166 and 1.217 for Membership Fees for UKPA (refer to Table 5.2) were not only significantly larger than the other two bodies, but also greater than the size of its Total Assets. This simple analysis not only illustrates the value of the AR methodology in directly benchmarking the performance of organisations, but also does so without requiring any form of currency conversions.

Anchored ratios and perspective scale

ARs are useful in assisting the assessment of the financial performance and growth of businesses. However, as they currently exist, these ratios do not readily enable the comparison of different businesses in a manner that instantly reflects any variations in perspective scale. The case study for the professional associations will be used to demonstrate this aspect. While it was shown that AUSPA exhibited the greatest amount of growth in Total Assets (refer to Table 5.2), without knowing the actual base level it relates to, it is difficult to fully appreciate the significance of this result. In order to compare businesses in a relative manner, but at the same time indicate the actual difference in size, it would be very helpful if both the PAR and AR were expressed in relation to the absolute value of the Total Assets figure from which they were derived. Consequently, it is suggested that all of the information that an analyst may require to fully assess the significance of a result they wish to analyse, could be summarised through a very simple form of shorthand. An example of how this could be reported is illustrated by the format recommended in Annotation 5.1. A practical example of this suggested annotation is provided in Figure 5.5.

In the format defined by Annotation 5.1, the variable β represents the anchored growth ratio of the variable being assessed and A_0 the currency value of Total Assets in the base period of analysis. The notation n represents the number of periods over which the change occurred, and the notation y represents the period that was selected as the base period of the analysis. It is believed that this form of approach to describing the performance of a variable in the financial statements of any business will prove to be beneficial to anyone that wishes to report and compare the outcomes of their analysis. All of the information that an analyst may need to consider the performance of a variable would be contained in the suggested annotation.

Anchored ratio annotation

$$\beta(A_0)^{n(y)} \tag{A5.1}$$

To illustrate Annotation 5.1, values will be assigned to the variables that it contains to describe the growth of AUSPA that was determined from Tables 2.9 and 5.2 as follows:

Variable Summary:
$\quad \beta = 1.1262$ (Table 5.2)
$\quad A_0 = \$84,501,000$ (Table 2.9)
$\quad n = 1$
$\quad y = 2009$

The completion of the annotation is as follows:

$$= 1.1262(\$84,501,000)^{1(2009)}$$

Figure 5.5 An example of Annotation 5.1.

Anyone with an understanding of the format of Annotation 5.1 would be able to interpret the information provided in the example in Figure 5.6 as stating that the level of Total Assets for AUSPA in the final year of analysis (2010) was \$95,164,000. This figure represents an increase of 1.1262 (β) times the base value of Total Assets of \$84,501,000 (A_0) over a period of one year (n) from the base period of 2009 (t). In order to illustrate the value of presenting information in this format, the annotation was also applied to the results from all of the professional bodies selected for the case study and summarised in Table 5.3. When information is presented in this type of arrangement, it becomes very easy to ascertain the comparative performance of the businesses being assessed. The presentation of the information in the prescribed annotation format in Table 5.3 allows the *relativity* of the performance between the associations (or any other business for that matter) to be compared by the figures on the left side of the brackets. The ability to ascertain the existence and magnitude of differences in the *perspective* size between the organisations is facilitated by the values that are *within* the brackets. This would enable an analyst that reviews the information in Table 5.3 to derive some immediate context for the magnitude of the growth between the organisations.

This is important when comparing the performance of smaller organisations to much larger ones. It is much easier for smaller organisations to increase their total size by significant values (the size of the base issue) than it is for larger organisations. Although this may be a problem when comparing the overall growth of an organisation (in terms of assessing the *significance* of that increase), this does not impact the comparative value of the

Table 5.3 Annotation summary of the total asset growth of three professional bodies

Bank	Anchored Annotation
USPA	$0.9725\,(\$232{,}050{,}000{,}000\ USD)^{1(2009)}$
UKPA	$1.0344\,(\$31{,}957{,}000\ GBP)^{1(2009)}$
AUSPA	$1.1262\,(\$84{,}501{,}000\ AUD)^{1(2009)}$

AR system as a whole. The AR values for all of the different variables will still be just as comparable to other entities. Their direct relativity will still be just as quantifiable. It simply adds another level of insight to recognise the numerical value of the Total Asset base of the different organisations being compared.

The scaling of other anchored ratios

The use of the annotation format described for AR analysis in the previous section is not solely limited to the application of the explanation of the Total Assets variable. This form of reporting can be extended to variables other than Total Assets. Indeed, this technique would be far more valuable for users if the application of the annotation technique is extended to other variables. For example, an analyst could also use this method of annotation style descriptions when anchoring the remaining balance sheet variables. These could be calculated and expressed on an individual basis as a direct analysis of the base level Total Assets, in the same format that is prescribed in Annotation 5.1, demonstrated in Figure 5.5 and applied in Table 5.3. Examples of this are provided by the following annotations:

$$\text{Anchored Total Liabilities Growth} = \left(A_0\right)^{t(y)} \tag{A5.2}$$

$$\text{Anchored Introduced Capital Growth} = \hat{C}\beta\left(A_0\right)^{t(y)} \tag{A5.3}$$

$$\text{Anchored Retained Earnings Growth} = \pi^r\beta\left(A_0\right)^{t(y)} \tag{A5.4}$$

$$\text{Anchored Reserves Growth} = \varpi\beta\left(A_0\right)^{t(y)} \tag{A5.5}$$

It is important to note that the sum of the ratios described in Annotations 5.2–5.5 can never be greater than the anchored Total Assets ratio (Annotation 5.1).

Service-based businesses

It could be argued that a technique that anchors all variables to Total Assets would not be as valid for service-based businesses because they would be unlikely to have as many Fixed Assets as other businesses. The counter-argument to this claim is that although the resulting PAR and AR values would be expected to be significantly larger values than businesses that require an extensive capital infrastructure, it would nevertheless be just as valid. The reasoning for this is that it would be natural for service-based businesses to require much less start-up capital and physical infrastructure and, as a result, the returns on investment would subsequently be expected to be much higher. Furthermore, a greater reliance on labour resources would result in much higher wage ratios and it would not naturally follow that surpluses would be higher for service-based businesses just because their physical infrastructure needs were lower.

Case study: application of anchored ratio methodology to GM

The financial statements for General Motors (GM) for the period 2009–2011 reported in Figure 2.1 were utilised to illustrate the AR technique. This consisted of applying the formulae and approach defined in Equations 5.1–5.3 to the values reported in Figure 2.1. This process resulted in the AR values for the variables that are summarised in Figure 5.6. Although requiring a base value for calculation, the AR technique is still able to provide values for all variables in the first year (2009 for this example) of any analysis. In addition, the AR values in Figure 5.6 exactly replicate the proportions and rates of growth of the currency values from which they were derived. Furthermore, because the AR values are ratios, they are far more meaningful than the currency values from which they were derived. For instance, whereas it is difficult to determine how good the currency value of $4,939 million for the 2010 Operating Surplus of GM (refer to Figure 2.1) was, the AR equivalent of 0.0362 (from Figure 5.6) has an inherent context of the base value Total Assets of GM. This means that, for this specific variable, an analyst has an instant understanding of the traditional Return on Assets (ROA) ratio (albeit this calculation is on the assets of a different period). The *inherent* context for every value for every variable is an important characteristic for the AR methodology. This is because it allows an instant comprehension of the quality of a performance.

Another useful benefit of this characteristic is that it also ensures that every other variable will genuinely reflect its performance relative to every other variable and every other period. That is, there is an *internal* context for the ratio values determined by this method. As a result, not only can the measured magnitude of the changes in a variable value be reliably ascertained with this technique, but the *significance* of the change can also be determined instantly. The AR values that have been derived for GM will help to illustrate these benefits and characteristics. The first aspect that will be examined for the results presented in Figure 5.6 is the overall trading performance of GM over the period of analysis. This is best reflected by the Operating Income/(loss) variable in the trading statement portion of Figure 5.6.

	2009 AR	2010 AR	2011 AR
Trading Statement			
Revenue			
Automotive Sales	0.7674	0.9915	1.0922
GM Financial Revenue	0	0.0021	0.0103
Total Revenue	0.7674	0.9936	1.1026
Expenses			
Automotive Cost of Sales	0.8227	0.8714	0.9566
GM Financial Expenses	0	0.0011	0.0058
Automotive Selling, General & Admin	0.0893	0.084	0.0888
Other Automotive Expenses	0.0092	0.0009	0.0004
Goodwill Impairment	0	0	0.0094
Total Costs & Expenses	0.9211	0.9574	1.0611
Operating Income / (loss)	-0.1538	0.0362	0.0415
Balance Sheet			
Assets			
Automotive Current Assets	0.4347	0.3893	0.442
Automotive Non-Current Assets	0.5653	0.5496	0.5232
GM Financial Assets	0	0.0802	0.0957
Total Assets	1	1.0191	1.061
Liabilities			
Automotive Current Liabilities	0.3847	0.346	0.359
Automotive Non-Current Liabilities	0.4028	0.3465	0.3512
GM Finance Liabilities	0	0.054	0.0647
Total Liabilities	0.7876	0.7465	0.7749
Net Assets	0.2124	0.2726	0.2861
Equity	0.2124	0.2726	0.2861
Total Equity	0.2124	0.2726	0.2861

Figure 5.6 Anchored ratio values for GM (2009 to 2011)[a].
a Determined from data presented in Figure 2.1.

The growth in the Operating Income/(loss) for GM from an AR of −0.1538 in 2009 to 0.0362 in 2010 represented a phenomenal turnaround in performance in a short space of time (refer to Figure 5.6). This overall improvement in performance was achieved through a significant increase in Total Revenue from 0.7674 in 2009 to 0.9936 in 2010 while, simultaneously, controlling the growth of expenditure to 0.9574 in 2010 from a value of 0.9211 in 2009 (refer to Figure 5.6). Although the currency values also depict this change in fortunes, the AR values truly quantify the magnitude of this performance. Without the inherent context capabilities of the AR methodology, a currency increase in the Operating Income/(loss) for GM of $ 25,897 million (refer to Figure 2.2) in 2010 may, or may not, be a significant result. When viewed from the perspective of the AR values, however, a change in the Operating Income/(loss) value that represents 19 per cent of the 2009 Total Assets for GM ($136,295 million in Figure 2.1) can only be viewed as a remarkable achievement.

Unlike the vertical and PAR techniques, the AR method is capable of determining the growth for the Total Assets values for GM over time. For example, the application of the AR method to the results for GM reveals that, during the time of analysis, the Total Assets for GM only grew to 1.0191 in 2010 from the base value of 1.0000 in 2009 (refer to Figure 5.6). This suggests that the growth in revenue and improved profitability for GM were purely a result of enhanced (and therefore organic) performance. This is because the minimal growth in the Total Assets of GM in this time indicates that there were no major acquisitions or investments that could account for the additional revenue. In other words, the improved performance for GM was holistic.

The AR technique and comparison to other techniques for GM's financial performance

The company GM has been used in several chapters to demonstrate how different techniques view the financial performance of this business for the financial years 2009–2011. Of all of the techniques examined to this point in time, the AR analysis approach is the only method for which the ratios it produces accurately and *faithfully* represents the currency values for *every* single variable reported in the financial statements that are being analysed. This understanding is what allows an analyst to utilise AR values as though they 'were' currency, but in the knowledge that they have been normalised for direct comparison to any other set of converted financials. This benchmarking may be internal or external to the organisation.

One of the main advantages of the AR technique over many of the other methods examined is that it is able to provide converted AR values for *every* currency value of financial variables for *every* period of analysis. The other methods examined have either not been able to provide a value for a period for a variable or not been able to provide a meaningful value for every variable. The latter is particularly true for the Total Assets variable. The AR technique is the only option of the techniques examined that can provide values that would reliably indicate the performance of Total Assets over time (currency provides values but does not contextualise the performance of this variable). Indeed, the only variable, and the only period, for which the AR technique will result in a base value of 1.0 (other variables and periods may also present this value by chance) will be the Total Assets variable for the first period of analysis. This is a major advancement over the VRA and PAR methods, which do not enable an assessment of growth and relative changes over time for this variable. This is because the ratio output for the Total Assets variable for both the VRA and PAR methods will be 1.0 for every period that is to be assessed.

In some cases, the other techniques examined to date can result in misleading impressions of performance. For example, under the percentage change and rolling period-to-period version of the horizontal trend analysis methods, the changes indicated for the income and expenses for the GM financial segment of the operations of GM were both reported as increasing by more than 400 per cent in 2011 (refer to Figure 3.1). This appears to be much more significant to GM than the reality that the revenue from this source only accounted for 1.03 per cent of the 2009 base-level Total Assets in terms of its AR in 2011 (refer to Figure 5.6). This example highlights how the AR method of analysis indicates the significance of a variable, in a manner that reflects its actual level of importance for the business as a whole, better than the percentage change (and horizontal change) method. Although, fundamentally, the percentage values that were over 400 per cent are mathematically sound, they could portray a very misleading message to management and investors when assessing the financial performance of the business.

This could be particularly detrimental if management were rewarded for their performance based on percentage change key performance indicators (KPIs). For example, would it be fair if the manager of the GM financial segment of the operations of GM received a bonus commensurate with a 400 per cent increase in revenue, when the currency value only represented around one per cent of the 2009 Total Asset value? Would this be further justified if the manager of the automotive division was not as well rewarded because they could 'only' manage a comparatively less impressive increase of around 10 per cent? If this was the case, the manager of the automotive division could be justifiably upset, given that the 10 per cent increase in this instance represented around $13.7 billion (Figure 2.2) and 99 per cent of Total Income.

Anchored ratio analysis of the GM financial segment

The PAR technique was used in Chapter 4 to examine the performance of the GM financial segment of their operations. In this chapter, the AR method will be used to explore the performance of that segment. The GM financial segment was specifically selected because the other techniques applied to date have not been capable of providing an assessment that matched the quality and the significance of the performance of this segment for the operations of GM *as a whole*. This analysis commences with an examination of the income variable for this specific segment. When viewed in isolation of all of the other activities for GM, the growth in the numerical currency values for GM financial income from zero in 2009 to $1,410 million in 2011 (refer to Figure 2.1) could appear to be very impressive. As identified in Chapter 2, however, the level of the growth in the numerical currency value of the GM's financial income could be quite deceptive without the comparative context of the values from other sources of income to indicate the internal perspective scale of this variable.

The AR technique renders the need for relative context for financial performance measurement purposes obsolete. Because AR values possess the characteristic of inherent context, there is no need for an analyst to concern themselves with the level of significance of the results they are reviewing. This is because there can be no mistaking the reported AR values in Figure 5.6 for GM Financial Revenue of 0, 0.0021 and 0.0103, for the years 2009–2011, respectively, as being anything other than relatively insignificant for the operations of GM in general. The underlying ARs of 0.0021 for 2010 GM financial income and 0.0103 for 2011 GM financial income (as per Figure 5.6) indicate that this segment does not reflect a sizeable proportion of Total Revenue in comparison to the Total Assets for GM. This is determinable from the AR values no matter how impressive the currency values or the mathematical percentage change calculation may be for the increase in GM financial income.

These conclusions for the GM financial income are very different from that which would be determined for income from their predominant revenue earning segment of automotive production and sales through the use of the AR methodology. Although the Total Assets for GM increased from the 2009 base value of 1.0000 to the AR value of 1.0191 in 2010, the automotive sales revenue for GM increased over this same time from an AR in 2009 of 0.7675 to a ratio of 0.9915 (refer to Figure 5.6). This means that although the Total Asset value for GM only increased by 1.91 per cent of the 2009 base value of Total Assets, the automotive sales revenue increased by roughly 23 per cent of its 2009 Total Asset base value in the same time period (refer to Figure 5.6).

The percentage change for automotive sales in 2011 was 10.16 per cent (refer to Figure 3.1). This compares to a percentage increase of 401.78 for GM's financial revenue for the same period (refer to Figure 3.1). This would suggest that the GM financial segment significantly outperformed the automotive segment. The AR changes for these variables in 2011 were an increase of 0.1007 for automotive sales and 0.0082 for GM financial revenue (refer to Figure 5.6). The percentage change results suggest that the performance for the GM financial segment was the most impressive of the two segments. On the other hand, the AR results demonstrate that, in terms of the significance for GM as a business, the automotive segment outperformed the GM financial segment by around 12 times the impact.

The magnitude of this achievement is further highlighted by the review of the ARs for the relevant expense categories for GM. The ARs for the expenses of the GM financial segment of GM's operations once again indicate that management would hardly be concerned by values of 0.0011 for 2009 and 0.0058 in 2011 (refer to Figure 5.6). The results for GM's automotive operations, on the other hand, are more impressive. Although the ARs for automotive sales increased significantly in 2010, the AR of 0.8714 for the cost of sales for this segment in 2010 only increased by 0.05 over its 2009 counterpart value in the same period of time (refer to Figure 5.6). When the revenue and expenses of GM are considered in tandem, their respective AR values demonstrate that there was quite a significant increase in the profitability of the business. Further analysis determines that the automotive sales operations of GM were primarily responsible for this improvement. Indeed, these results clarify how GM was able to turn an Operating Loss with an AR of −0.1538 in 2009 into an Operating Profit AR value of 0.0362 in 2010 (refer to Figure 5.6).

Of course, this form of analysis does not need to be limited to the trading statement variables and can be extended to other financial variables such as Liabilities and Net Assets. The ARs for the GM Financial Assets for GM increased from 0.0802 in 2010 to 0.0957 in 2011 (refer to Figure 5.6). During the same time frame, the GM Financial Liabilities increased from 0.0540 in 2009 to 0.0647 in 2011 (refer to Figure 5.6). The differences between these variables for the two different financial years show that this new segment of operations helped to increase the overall Net Asset position of GM. The values that were determined for the Net Assets of GM financial operations for the 2010 and 2011 financial years will, of course, result in the ability to ascertain the changes in the return on Net Assets for those years. In 2010, with an Operating Profit AR of 0.0010 and a Net Assets AR of 0.0262 (refer to Figure 5.6), the return on Net Assets for this segment was 3.82 per cent. This compares to a rate of 14.52 per cent that was generated in 2011 from a Gross Profit margin AR of 0.0045 in comparison to the Net Asset AR value of 0.0310 (refer to Figure 5.6).

Case study: anchored ratios for Australian banks

As the process of ARs is an extension of the process for PARs, this case study will advance on the case study material for Australian banks in Chapter 4. Because the 2006 financial year will form the base year for this example, and keeping in mind that the application of the AR method in the base year will be identical to the PAR application for that period, the AR values for this base year are identical to the values reported in Table 4.3. In order to calculate the ARs for the 2007 financial year of the four banks in this example, it will be necessary to utilise the currency values for the 2006 Total Assets variable contained in Table 4.2 as the base for the anchoring process. Using the guidance of Equations 5.1–5.3, *all* of the currency values for the financial variables for the 2007 financial year contained in Table 4.4 were converted into AR values. Anchored to the 2006 financial year Total Asset values in Table 4.2, the 2007 AR values for this case study are summarised in Table 5.4.

Table 5.4 Anchored ratios of four Australian banks for 2007 financial year

Variable	CBA	NAB	WBC	BOQ
	A_0	A_0	A_0	A_0
Income	0.0899	0.0917	0.0866	0.0943
Operating Profit	0.0363	0.0331	0.034	0.0317
Assets	1.1518	1.1657	1.2512	1.2684
Liabilities	1.0856	1.1031	1.1659	1.2143
Introduced Capital	0.0418	0.0263	0.0264	0.039
Retained Earnings	0.0172	0.0331	0.0324	0.0096
Reserves	0.0058	0.0022	0.0006	0.0055

A_0 = Ratios for 2007 financial year are anchored to the 2006 Total Assets values in Table 4.4.

It has been shown that for reasons that include the impact of the phenomenon of perspective scale and a lack of inherent context, there can be no instant determinations of the quality of the performance of a financial variable reported in currency values. The same cannot be said for AR values. One of the benefits of the AR analysis methodology is that the extent, and more importantly, the significance of any value through the outputs of the AR technique should be readily apparent. Possessing all of the benefits of the PAR technique, including an identical ability to normalise the information being assessed, the AR technique also has the additional benefit of enabling an assessment of the growth in the Total Assets variable. For example, although the PAR methodology would have resulted in values of 1.0 for the 2007 Assets variables for the four banks, the AR method will produce values that also reflect the change in the size of the variable for all of the banks being examined.

The AR values in Table 5.4 enable any analyst to ascertain that every bank in this example managed to increase its Assets. More importantly, the AR values for this variable enable an analyst to determine the relative *quality* of each performance for this variable in a manner that is not available from the other methods examined to date. For example, it can be instantly determined that, with an AR value of 1.2684 for Assets in Table 5.4, BOQ experienced the greatest level of growth for this variable from its 2006 base. This ability, or characteristic, of inherent context, allows an analyst to validly compare the AR for any financial variable value to any other value within or external to an organisation. For example, it is also apparent that with a value of 0.0943 (refer to Table 5.4), BOQ generated the highest AR value for Income of the four banks for the 2007 financial year. Despite having the lowest level of growth in Assets (with an AR value of 1.1518 in Table 5.4) and the second lowest AR value for Income (with an AR value of 0.0899 in Table 5.4), CBA managed to report the largest AR value for Operating Profit. Although the claim could be made on the Operating Profit AR value of 0.0363 for CBA alone (refer to Table 5.4), the additional information demonstrates that CBA was, overall, the best-performing bank of the four banks for 2007.

Assessment of the AR methodology

Of all of the techniques examined, the AR methodology is the only one that overcomes the issues identified in Chapter 1 without being susceptible to other deficiencies. The AR method overcomes perspective scale, issues of currency conversion, temporal consistency and context. It also provides values for every period of analysis and even allows assessments to be made for every single variable in the financial statements. It achieves all of this while possessing a linear relationship to the currency values from which the AR values are derived. Because the AR values have an inherent context, an AR value can instantly convey significance and comparability.

A potential criticism of the technique may be that the data from which the AR (and PAR) method determine their values could be suspect due to accounting policies, principles and conventions. A counter-claim to this suggestion is that all numerical financial performance measurement systems are inherently reliant upon the quality of the data presented in financial statements. If the data being analysed is flawed, then no technique will be able to overcome this deficiency.

Other claims of deficiencies may be related to an inability for the proposed system of PAR and AR values to be unable to overcome changes in accounting principles and policies. In any case, although the accounting principles that dictate financial reporting requirements may change over time (and therefore normally create problems for studies in relation to the comparability of data), the ratios generated by this system for any given year will be valid for that year (particularly for PAR outputs) and would compare across time periods in the same way that they would compare between different businesses. In terms of the AR methodology, this problem could also be overcome (but is not necessarily required) by resetting the period that the data is being anchored to.

It may be that other shortcomings of this technique be discovered over time. Despite this possibility, however, the superior levels of reliability and comparability that this system provides in comparison to other available techniques should provide users of the system with a great deal of insight and utility. Indeed, because it overcomes the issues that render other techniques fundamentally flawed, the AR method should be considered the best method for financial performance measurement, assessment and benchmarking.

Summary

It was shown in Chapter 4 that currency values for financial variables could be converted into meaningful ratios by deriving proportional values for them against the Total Asset variable value for each period. This chapter advanced on the development of the PAR method with the development of the AR methodology. This involved anchoring the conversion of currency values for financial variables to the Total Assets value of a base period of analysis. This chapter also illustrated the additional benefits that were available from this difference from the PAR technique. These benefits included the ability to derive values for the Total Assets variable over time and also the fact that the resulting ratios for all of the variables matched the patterns of growth for those variables over time. There were no major criticisms identified for this technique at this time.

References

AUSPA, 2010. CPA Australia Annual Report 2010.

BOQ, 2006. BOQ Bank of Queensland Annual Report 2006.

CBA, 2006. Commonwealth Bank of Australia Annual Report 2006.

GM, 2009. GM Annual Report 2009.

GM, 2010. GM Annual Report 2010.

GM, 2011. GM Annual Report 2011.

NAB, 2006. NAB National Australia Bank Annual Financial Report 2006.

Pike, S. and Roos, G., 2007. The Validity of Measurement Frameworks. In: A. Neely, ed. *Business Performance Measurement: Unifying Theories and Integrating Practices.* Cambridge: Cambridge University Press, pp. 218–237.

UKPA, 2010. CIMA Chartered Institute of Management Accountants, Financial Statements 2010.

USPA, 2010. AICPA American Institute of CPAs, Annual Report 2010.

WBC, 2006. Westpac Annual Financial Report 2006.

6 Integrated ratio analysis

Abstract

Having developed the proportional asset ratio (PAR) technique in Chapter 4 and the anchored ratio (AR) technique in Chapter 5, this chapter demonstrated how the simultaneous application of the two approaches over time represented the complete integrated ratio analysis method (IRAM) advocated for in this book. The combined use of the AR and PAR techniques that form the IRAM as a system ensures that the advantages of each technique are maximised and any negative issues minimised. After describing how the complete methodology would work in practice, this chapter provided some important examples of how the system could help to generate significant business and competitive intelligence to assist management to better manage their organisations.

The adoption and implementation of the IRAM would be very simple for organisations to achieve. The direct benefits of more focused decision-making by managers from this objective would be improved financial performance and more sustainable operations. If an organisation is in a market that is open to economic competition (e.g. not a government agency), and the financial statements of that entity are publicly available, it would be possible for the competitors to conduct competitive intelligence of their own using the IRAM. This could reveal operational deficiencies and weaknesses that they could exploit and target in their strategic objectives. Therefore, it would be prudent that, at a minimum, your organisation is aware of what your financials could be revealing to your competitors if they use this system against your organisation.

Introduction

The previous chapters have detailed how current techniques for financial performance measurement analysis and benchmarking are unable to fully satisfy the purpose for which they are employed. The issues that result in this scenario were also identified and explored. Later chapters have presented a new algorithm that can be employed in two different temporal approaches that overcome the issues identified for the other methodologies. This chapter will explore the additional insight that can be generated and provided to analysts by the simultaneous utilisation of the proportional asset ratio (PAR) and the anchored ratio (AR) into the integrated ratio analysis method (IRAM).

The integrated ratio analysis method

The simultaneous combined use of the PAR and AR techniques forms the integrated ratio analysis method (IRAM). The actual practice of implementing the IRAM simply involves the overlay of the results of the PAR and AR analysis for any particular variables over a number of periods. It is noted that for the very first period of application of the PAR or AR method, the results for every single variable will be *exactly* the same. If there are any changes to the value of Total Assets after this period, then the values from the application of PAR and AR will diverge. Apart from the PAR value for the Total Assets variable (which will always be 1.0 for every period of application), if the value of a variable deviates (positively *or* negatively) from the base value, then there has been a *real* or 'holistic' change in the value of that variable. This differs from a reflection of the numerical growth of a variable, which is replicated by the AR values.

It was shown in earlier chapters that the larger the size of an organisation (in terms of Total Assets), the larger the values for Income and Operating Result were likely to be. If, therefore, an organisation grows during a period because it has acquired a new business, for example, then it is most likely that the Income and Operating Result should have increased numerically simply because the organisation was now larger. As a result, changes in the structural base of a business, such as this example, may obscure the financial performance of the business. If, however, an analyst concurrently utilises the PAR and AR methods in their assessment of financial performance, then a real insight into whether the changes in the variable values of financial statements were subject to *real* growth can be ascertained. In other words, a conclusion can be made as to whether the values for the variables have been affected as a consequence of a change in size.

In order to illustrate the practical application of the IRAM, the information for the hypothetical profit analysis will be utilised again. In order to better illustrate the system, however, additional information will be needed. For this example, values will be provided for Total Assets that will equate to the same values as those for the hypothetical profit. The application of both the PAR and AR techniques in this example will then be in compliance with the actual design of the system. The currency values for Profit and Total Assets and also the AR and PAR calculations for the Profit variable for this example are reported in Table 6.1.

Table 6.1 Hypothetical profit sequence and anchored and proportional asset ratios

Time (t)	1	2	3	4	5	6	7
Profit ($π)	100	110	120	130	140	150	160
AR (π)	1.00	1.10	1.20	1.30	1.40	1.50	1.60
PAR (π)	1.00	1.00	1.00	1.00	1.00	1.00	1.00
Total Assets	100	110	120	130	140	150	160

The AR and PAR values for the example in Table 6.1 are depicted in Figure 6.1. As expected, the AR values directly represent the currency values for profit in a perfectly linear relationship. This means that the AR values indicate the growth trajectory of the currency values of the variable in a normalised manner over time. The PAR values for the Profit variable in the example in Table 6.1, however, present a straight-line trajectory that is perfectly horizontal. The PAR values indicate that the 'growth' in the numerical values of the variable is not 'organic' or 'real'. That is, although the increasing values of Total Assets indicate that the business in this example has been 'growing' over time (and the AR values for Profit have also grown), the constant PAR values for the Profit variable indicate that this variable has been growing in exactly the same proportion as the Total Assets (business).

This means that the numerical growth in the Profit variable does not represent a change in the *actual* performance. While this example does not represent a 'bad' performance history, what an analyst would prefer to see in this example would be no discrepancy between the AR and PAR values at all. This scenario would indicate that the growth for the Profit variable has been *entirely* attributable to changes in performance and not perspective

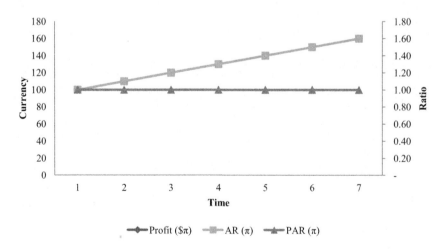

Figure 6.1 The application of the IRAM to hypothetical profits in Table 6.1.

scale. It is this vital understanding that illustrates the ultimate power and insight available through the use of the IRAM. If an investor wants to invest in the option which would return the best value for their money, they would use this system to compare the investment options that they have before them. If management want to ensure that their organisation is performing at the optimum levels that they are able to achieve, then they would use this system to help inform their decisions.

Using integrated ratio analysis to identify issues

The Australian Stock Exchange (ASX) listed company, ABC Learning, was identified in Chapter 1 as an example of a business that had been reporting outstanding traditional financial performance metrics but had still failed unexpectedly. It was also stated in Chapter 1 that the use of a system such as the IRAM would have alerted management and investors of the issues that caused the failure a great deal earlier than it actually became apparent. Used as a case study to illustrate various techniques and issues to date, the business General Motors (GM) will be used as a benchmark comparison to ABC Learning to illustrate the benefits of the IRAM for managers, investors and other stakeholders. For this purpose, some representative Operating Surplus values for GM (2009 to 2011) and ABC Learning (2004 to 2007) were converted into AR ratios and illustrated in Figure 6.2. The AR technique faithfully replicates the growth rates of financial variables over time, while simultaneously normalising those results. Consequently, the direct comparison of the AR values for the Operating Surplus variable between these companies demonstrates just how phenomenal the performance of ABC Learning appeared to be (refer to Figure 6.2). With results such as these, it is little wonder that investors flocked to this company during that time.

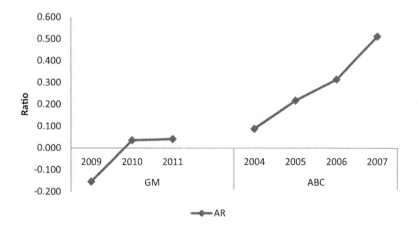

Figure 6.2 AR comparison of operating result for GM and ABC Learning.

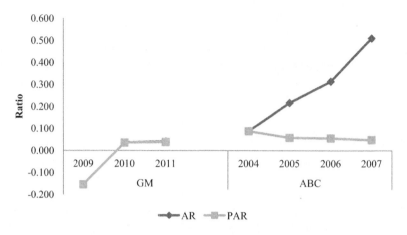

Figure 6.3 IRAM application to operating result for GM and ABC Learning.

Once the PAR values of this variable are overlayed against the AR values (as per Figure 6.3), however, a much different view of the performance of ABC Learning is revealed. Given that the PAR values for the Operating Surplus for GM are almost identical to their AR values for the same period of time, it is apparent that the growth rates for this variable for GM were mostly organic (refer to Figure 6.3). The results for ABC Learning, however, are in very stark contrast to those of GM. From the results depicted in Figure 6.3, it is quite apparent that the difference between the AR and PAR values in the time period of analysis was becoming extremely divergent. This suggests that the apparently 'phenomenal' performance of ABC Learning was more likely a result of perspective-scale growth. This is reflected in the Annual Reports of ABC Learning, where it was revealed that this company was on a very aggressive strategy of acquisitions.

In itself, this strategy should not have been a factor in the eventual demise of ABC Learning. If ABC Learning was able to at least maintain the PAR value at a perfectly horizontal rate, then the performance it would have been achieving would have been consistent with maintaining the *actual* level of performance (where it was sustainable) as the business continued to expand. Over this time frame, however, the PAR values for the Operating Surplus variable for ABC Learning were actually declining. This knowledge would have armed management and investors with the insight to more closely scrutinise the financial performance and strategies of ABC Learning to possibly avoid the sudden failure.

Using integrated ratio analysis to develop budgets and set performance targets

The establishment of performance metrics and related targets to be met can assist an organisation to aim for aspirational performance. How performance targets are established can have a significant (and possibly unintentionally negative) impact on the future of an organisation. The use of the hypothetical profits example adopted in previous illustrations can help to demonstrate this. If a firm generates an increase in profit of 10 currency units more than the base of $100 in year one, the management may thereafter set a target increase of 10 per cent per annum to match this performance. Assuming that Profit continues to increase by the same 10 currency units per annum, the percentage change of these increases will reduce as the base value continues to increase (refer to Table 6.1). This may leave management with the impression that performance is declining and they could introduce measures (such as firing managers) to try and 'improve' performance.

If, indeed, management set a performance target of a constant increase in profit of 10 per cent per annum, an unintended consequence of a goal such as this is that an increasing base value will compound the effects of the required target. This is also demonstrated in Table 6.2, where the Target Profit values in the last row have been set as a 10 per cent increase over the previous periods' result. Comparing the Target Profit values to the Profit values in the first row shows that a compounding target of 10 per cent will require 17 more currency units to be achieved in Period 7 than the organisation may have otherwise naturally (sustainably) achieved (refer to Table 6.2). A compounding percentage target can result in undue pressure on managers to achieve revenue targets beyond what is holistically achievable. Alternatively, management may introduce expenditure cuts that could actually damage the business to meet the imposed target.

If management want to set targets that do not have an unintended compounding effect, they could use the AR system to establish goals that are more holistically achievable. It could be, for example, that management determine that constant increases of 10 currency units is the safest achievable target and use the AR system to develop targets such as the AR values reported in Table 5.1. It would be recommended that once AR targets have been proposed by management (accounting for expected numerical growth), the IRAM process should be completed by applying the PAR technique to those projected values to ensure that the expected growth is, in fact, organic. The aim of this exercise would be to ensure that the difference between the two values (AR and PAR) is as small as possible. This is a good way to ensure that any 'stretch' targets are actually achievable.

One of the key implications of an organisation utilising the IRAM for establishing future performance metrics is that it encourages longer-term

Table 6.2 Hypothetical profit sequence and comparison to target profit at 10% increase

Time (t)	1	2	3	4	5	6	7
Profit (π)	100.00	110.00	120.00	130.00	140.00	150.00	160.00
% Change (%Δ)	–	10.00	9.10	8.30	7.70	7.10	6.70
Target Profit (+10%)	100	110	121	133	146	161	177

vision and planning. An over-reliance on short- to medium-term metrics and review such as monthly, or yearly, is what may inadvertently create the compounding performance expectations. The use of the IRAM for establishing budgets and performance metrics is, of course, not limited to the profit variable. It should also be used to help with budgeting revenue, expenditure and all other trading statement and balance sheet items. There needs to be an understanding that the trading statement and the balance sheet are inextricably linked and that performance planning and analysis must view this relationship as such when those processes are being conducted. The use of the Profit variable in this section was merely an example of why it needs to be done and the benefits of utilising the IRAM for these purposes.

Using integrated ratio analysis for monthly reports and forecasting

The IRAM is not limited to the analysis and preparation of reporting and budgeting processes for annual time frames. It can also be used to assist with monthly (or even more frequent) reporting of actual results and variances to budget. Indeed, the more often it is used, the more likely that management can better control the deviations between the AR and PAR values of different variables on a timelier basis. In an age where managers and decision-makers are inundated with information overload, it is more important than ever to be able to focus on areas that have the most impact. The IRAM will produce outputs that will better reflect the significance of changes to financial variables. Consequently, the use of the IRAM to report variances to budget (instead of currency or percentage values) will also assist management to focus on the variances that are actually significant.

Variances help to inform management where their original projections have not come to pass and, thereby, rest their expectations through the development of forecasts. These forecasts will take into account whether these variances are merely an unexpected one-off occurrence or a continuing change to the operations of a business. The IRAM could be utilised in this process to help develop the forecast for the changed conditions. If, for example, the budget for revenue for a period was significantly under- or over-estimated, then the expenditure parameters for managers (forecasts and revised budgets) can be reset and tested through the IRAM to ensure the impact of this variation is minimised or maximised as applicable.

Integrated ratio analysis as a tool for business intelligence

Although it was originally developed for the primary purpose of enabling superior benchmarking analysis of the financial performance of different businesses, this system is more than capable of providing insights into the operations of a single business that may not be possible from other forms of analysis. One of the main benefits of the IRAM is that it is a system that is not confined to profit-maximising entities to be effective. The nature of the system and how it works ensures that the operating result from trading is not the main variable of focus to assess the financial performance of an organisation. Melbourne Water (MW) was selected as the organisation that would assist the illustration of how this system could be utilised to generate some internal business intelligence (BI). MW is a statutory authority owned by the Victorian government. Its primary purpose is to provide water, sewerage treatment and manage waterways (Melbourne Water, 2020, p. 2).

The analysis will start with three main trading statement variables as a high-level overview of the application of the IRAM in comparison to traditional techniques. The variables selected include the Total Revenue, Total Expenses and Net Result Before Tax for the period 2009–2013. The currency values and graphical presentation of this information is provided in Figure 6.4, which shows a generally positive pattern of growth in the Revenue and Net Result values for MW until an obvious increase in the 2013 Total Expenses resulted in a loss for that period. What this analysis doesn't reveal, however, is the quality of the performance of each period relative to other periods. How do we *know* if one period's performance was better than another? Traditional approaches that have attempted to resolve this issue have included the technique of determining the change in the currency value of the variables from one period to another (Figure 6.5). Analysing financial data in terms of the changes in the currency values of the variables undoubtedly provides useful information. The information presented in Figure 6.5, for example, suggests that the general improvement in performance of the variables assessed may not have been as consistent as it appears on a prima-facie basis.

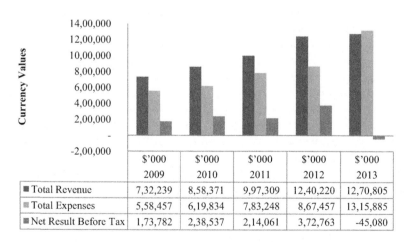

	$'000 2009	$'000 2010	$'000 2011	$'000 2012	$'000 2013
■ Total Revenue	7,32,239	8,58,371	9,97,309	12,40,220	12,70,805
■ Total Expenses	5,58,457	6,19,834	7,83,248	8,67,457	13,15,885
■ Net Result Before Tax	1,73,782	2,38,537	2,14,061	3,72,763	-45,080

Figure 6.4 Currency values for Melbourne Water trading variables for 2009–2013.

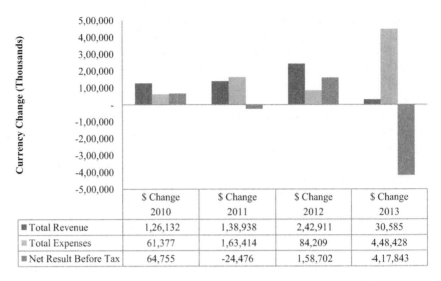

	$ Change 2010	$ Change 2011	$ Change 2012	$ Change 2013
■ Total Revenue	1,26,132	1,38,938	2,42,911	30,585
▦ Total Expenses	61,377	1,63,414	84,209	4,48,428
■ Net Result Before Tax	64,755	-24,476	1,58,702	-4,17,843

Figure 6.5 Currency change values for Melbourne Water trading variables for 2009–2013.

Percentage changes applied to Melbourne Water financial variables

The changes in currency for the results for MW for 2009–2013 (in Figure 6.5) were converted into percentage change values (refer to Figure 6.6). One of the major deficiencies of the percentage change technique is that, when the individual calculation of changes is performed in isolation of other changes in a data set of more than one variable, the relative significance of the changes can be appreciably distorted. In Figure 6.6, for example, the percentage change in the Net Result for 2010 (37 per cent) was more than twice the size of the percentage change in Total Revenue (17 per cent) when the currency change of the Net Result ($64,755 as per Figure 6.5) was only around half of the currency change for Total Revenue ($126,132 as per Figure 6.5).

This distortion of comparability is significantly magnified in the 2012 financial year. The percentage change for the Net Result in 2012 for MW was a 74 per cent increase (refer to Figure 6.6). This value is *three* times greater than the percentage change value for Total Revenue (24 per cent in Figure 6.6). This is despite the currency value of the change in Net Result was only 65 per cent of the currency value change of Total Revenue for 2012 (refer to Figure 6.6). Finally, the percentage change of the Net Result for 2013 (−112 per cent as per Figure 6.6) was more than double the percentage change in Total Expenses (52 per cent as per Figure 6.6) *despite* the currency change in Total Expenses (Figure 6.5) being *larger* than the change in the Net Result (taking into account that the Net Result change was negative).

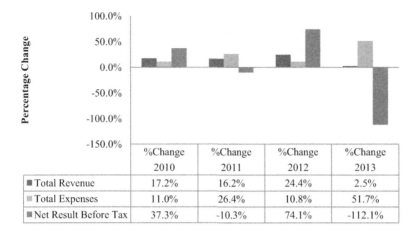

Figure 6.6 Percentage change values for Melbourne Water trading variables for 2009–2013.

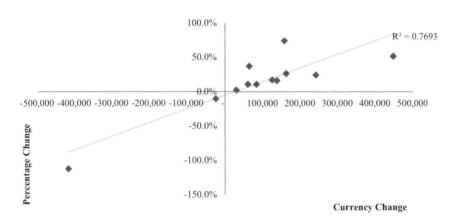

Figure 6.7 Relationship between percentage and currency value changes for Melbourne Water trading variables for 2009–2013.

The extent of the deficiencies of the percentage change technique in an environment where there is multiple variables in a single data set is well illustrated by Figure 6.7. If a measurement scale accurately portrays the characteristics of the aspect being measured, then the relationship between the scale and the element being measured should be linear. Although the relationship for the percentage change values to the currency change values for MW appears to be fairly linear (at an R^2 of 0.7693 in Figure 6.7), there are still many outliers that are more consistent with what has been observed for commercial business entities. The fact that the exhibited relationship for

MW is considerably more linear than those observed for private enterprise examples, suggests that governments and government agencies have greater control over their revenue and expenditure variations than their private enterprise counterparts. Nevertheless, this still demonstrates the unreliability that percentage change calculations have in relation to the confidence an analyst can place on their faithful representation of the significance of the changes in performance that percentage changes purport to represent.

The anchored ratio technique applied to Melbourne Water financial variables

The application of the AR technique to the currency values presented in Figure 6.4 is provided in Figure 6.8. As explained in Chapter 5, these values replicate the currency value patterns perfectly while simultaneously converting them into normalised ratio values. The similarity between Figure 6.4 to Figure 6.8 demonstrates how the AR technique achieves this. The difference is that while there is no inherent context for the currency values presented in Figure 6.4, the AR values in Figure 6.8 do possess this characteristic. The currency value of $214,068 for the 2011 Net Result Before Tax variable in Figure 6.4, for example, does *not* imply any outside reference to enable an analyst to determine the quality (or magnitude) of that result. On the other hand, the AR value for this variable in Figure 6.8 *does* contain an inherent context. Any analyst would know that the AR value for the 2011 Net Result Before Tax variable in Figure 6.8 is 0.03949 of the *Total Assets* for MW. This provides an instant context of the magnitude and, therefore, quality of the result.

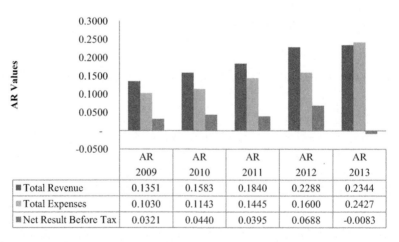

	AR 2009	AR 2010	AR 2011	AR 2012	AR 2013
■ Total Revenue	0.1351	0.1583	0.1840	0.2288	0.2344
▩ Total Expenses	0.1030	0.1143	0.1445	0.1600	0.2427
■ Net Result Before Tax	0.0321	0.0440	0.0395	0.0688	-0.0083

Figure 6.8 AR values for Melbourne Water trading variables for 2009–2013.

Furthermore, whereas the percentage change values for MW provided misleading indications of the significance of the changes in variable values relative to each other, the AR technique reflects the changes in the *exact* proportion that they occurred in the actual currency values (refer to Figure 6.9). This aspect is validated by Figure 6.10, which, unlike the relationship between percentage and currency changes depicted in Figure 6.7, the relationship between the AR ratio and currency changes is perfectly linear (at an R^2 of 1.0). Because of this relationship, the values depicted in Figures 6.8 and 6.9 enable an analyst to appreciate and rely upon the significance of the

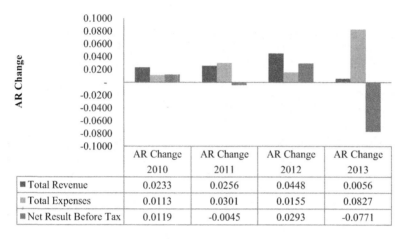

	AR Change 2010	AR Change 2011	AR Change 2012	AR Change 2013
■ Total Revenue	0.0233	0.0256	0.0448	0.0056
▨ Total Expenses	0.0113	0.0301	0.0155	0.0827
■ Net Result Before Tax	0.0119	-0.0045	0.0293	-0.0771

Figure 6.9 AR change values for Melbourne Water trading variables for 2009–2013.

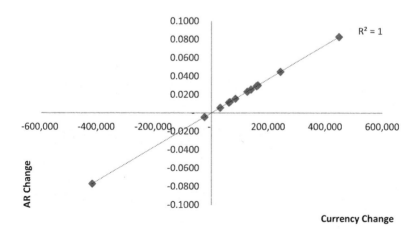

Figure 6.10 Relationship between AR and currency value changes for Melbourne Water trading variables for 2009–2013.

outputs provided. For example, from the application of this method, not only is the change in the Net Result Before Tax AR ratio for 2010 (0.0119 in Figure 6.9) around half the value of that for Total Revenue (0.0233 in Figure 6.9), it is also around the same value as that determined for Total Expenses (0.0113 in Figure 6.9). This is far a more accurate representation of the magnitude of the change and the significance of the change to the entire data set than what was determined by using the percentage change technique.

The proportional asset ratio technique applied to Melbourne Water financial variables

Whereas the AR methodology will replicate the patterns of currency values for financial variables over time, the PAR methodology will convert those amounts into values that represent the performance of those variables for one specific period. This allows an analyst to determine whether the performance of one period was better or worse than any other period. That is, it compares each period as though they are from a separate business and therefore eliminate issues of *internal* scale. The PAR values for the select financial variables for MW are presented in Figure 6.11. A comparison of the results in Figure 6.11 to those of Figures 6.4 and 6.8 will show that the PAR results present a very different impression of the financial performance of MW than either the currency (Figure 6.4) or AR values (Figure 6.11) indicate. Whereas, for example, the 2009 Total Revenue values for currency and AR formats are the lowest values of the five-year period of analysis, the PAR value in Figure 6.11 is actually the highest (or best) value for the period. Furthermore, there appears to have been a dramatic change in the financial

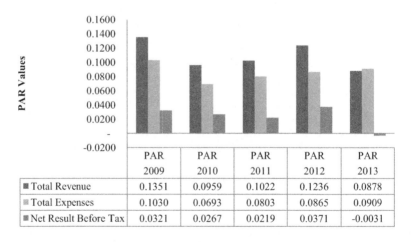

	PAR 2009	PAR 2010	PAR 2011	PAR 2012	PAR 2013
■ Total Revenue	0.1351	0.0959	0.1022	0.1236	0.0878
▨ Total Expenses	0.1030	0.0693	0.0803	0.0865	0.0909
■ Net Result Before Tax	0.0321	0.0267	0.0219	0.0371	-0.0031

Figure 6.11 PAR values for Melbourne Water trading variables for 2009–2013.

performance of MW in 2010, after which the performance of Total Revenue resumed an upward trajectory, until the 2013 financial year. This insight into the 'holistic' performance of MW would not be as available from traditional methods.

The integrated ratio analysis methodology applied to Melbourne Water financial variables

Measuring two completely different aspects of financial performance, the IRAM provides its maximum benefit when both techniques are used simultaneously. As the AR technique demonstrates the actual pattern of growth of a specific variable over time, by overlaying these outputs over the information provided by the PAR method, an analyst can determine whether this pattern of growth is organic (i.e. it is a result of business as usual trading and not an outcome of some other significant factor affecting the nature of the operations). The analysis of the revenue generated by MW is the perfect example. The AR patterns for the three revenue variables for MW in Figure 6.12 demonstrate that the Total Sales Revenue for MW almost doubled over the period of analysis, while the growth for the other two categories stagnated. Overlaid against the PAR values for the same time period, however, demonstrates that the holistic growth for the Total Sales Revenue variable for MW actually *fell* over this period of time (refer to Figure 6.12). Indeed, the discrepancy between the AR and PAR values for this variable over the time frame of analysis indicates that there were dramatic variations in performance for MW.

Given the dramatic variance in the AR and PAR values for the Total Sales Revenue variable in Figure 6.12, the insight from this analysis can

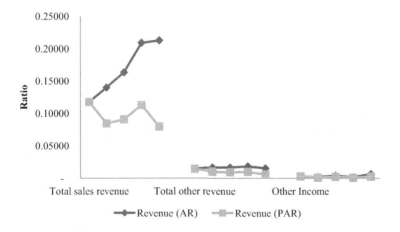

Figure 6.12 IRAM applied to Melbourne Water revenue variables for 2009–2013.

be improved by utilising the 'forwards and backwards' abilities of the AR technique and changing the year selected for the base value. Instead of anchoring the information for MW to the Total Assets of the first period of data in the sample (2009), for example, the base year was changed to 2010. As demonstrated by the resulting Figure 6.13, the performance of MW over the time frame examined highlights the years 2009 and 2013 as being outliers in performance rather than a consistently significant decline in performance for the variable overall. A comparison of Figures 6.12 and 6.13 also show that 2009 and 2013 were similar outlier years for the Total Other Revenue variable for MW.

A review of the Annual Reports for MW revealed that there was a revaluation in the value of assets for the organisation in 2010. This explains the divergence in the methods from the 2009 financial year and justifies the use of the forwards and backwards adjustment to the base period for this example. This alteration confirms that the growth for 2010 and 2011 for the revenue variables was, indeed, predominantly organic. A similar review of the 2013 Annual Reports for MW revealed that there was a transfer of the Victorian Desalination Plant to MW in 2013. The use of the combined techniques in Figure 6.13 indicates that the inclusion of the operations of the Desalination Plant in 2013 significantly reduced the financial performance of MW from what was apparent in the currency values. The adjusted analysis reveals that the divergence in the overall performance of MW was not a systemic issue that was flagging imminent demise (such as for ABC Learning). None of the traditional techniques examined herein are capable of helping to focus the investigations of an analyst on the underlying factors that influence the financial performance

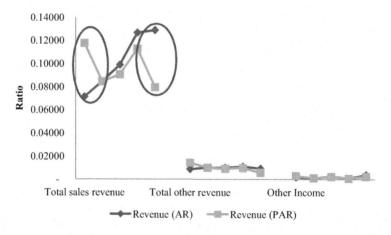

Figure 6.13 IRAM applied to Melbourne Water revenue variables for 2009–2013 – anchored to 2010 Total Assets.

of an organisation to the same extent. This demonstrates the utility of the IRAM to assist management with BI around their performance and strategic management.

The IRAM was also applied to the seven major categories of expenditure for MW for the period 2009–2013, and the results are shown in Figure 6.14. It can be concluded that, since the Depreciation, Operational and Finance Expense categories represent the largest expenditure items for MW, this is a business that is highly reliant upon its infrastructure. Furthermore, the significant spikes in the 2013 AR values for these three categories provide evidence to support the notion that the event that significantly affected the financial performance of MW was infrastructure related. This event was, of course, the transference of the operations of the Desalination Plant to MW. The results in Figure 6.14 also indicate that the category which was most significantly affected by the transference of the operations of the Desalination Plant was Finance Expenses. A more detailed analysis of the Finance Expenses category (in Figures 6.15 and 6.16) illustrates how significant the financing of the Desalination Plant has affected the operations of MW during this period. Overall, the internal analysis of the financial operations of MW has indicated that the most significant threat to its future performance is how the financing of Desalination Plant operations has been structured. The analysis of the results for MW for the period examined demonstrates the BI potential of this system. Although the analysis in this section has been performed on an annual time frame and using only actual information, this system would be even more useful when using it to analyse actual information in comparison to budgeted performance in real time.

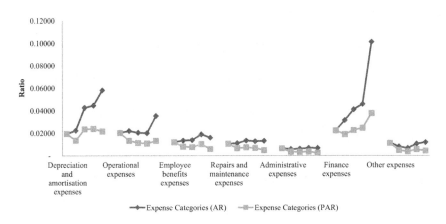

Figure 6.14 IRAM applied to Melbourne Water expense variables for 2009–2013.

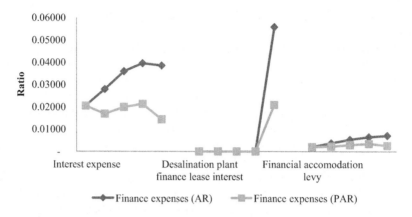

Figure 6.15 IRAM applied to Melbourne Water finance expenses variables for 2009–2013.

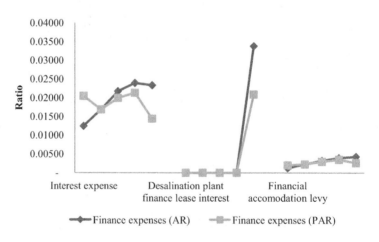

Figure 6.16 IRAM applied to Melbourne Water finance expenses variables for 2009–2013 – anchored to 2010 total assets.

Integrated ratio analysis as a tool for competitive intelligence

The development of the IRAM was aimed at overcoming the inability of traditional financial performance measurement techniques to enable valid benchmarking of different businesses. The resulting system not only enables this benchmarking to occur, but a skilled analyst could utilise the system to obtain competitive intelligence on its competitors. In order to illustrate the benchmarking and competitive intelligence capabilities of the system, the following businesses or government agencies (that predominantly operate in the supply of water) were selected for the analysis that follows:

Melbourne Water (MW), 2009 to 2013 – A Victorian government agency
Sydney Water (SW), 2009 to 2013 – A New South Wales government agency
South East Water Limited (SEW), 2009 to 2013 – An English water provider
 dealing in British pounds
Yarra Valley Water (YVW), 2009 to 2013 – A Victorian water retailer

The analysis commences with how the IRAM treats the Total Revenue values earned by the benchmarked businesses. The traditional currency values of the Total Revenue variable for these organisations are illustrated in Figure 6.17. This example demonstrates how disparate the four organisations are in terms of operational scale. This comparison is further complicated by the fact that the values for SEW are reported and depicted at their British currency values and have not been converted into Australian currency equivalents for this analysis. Apart from a visual depiction of variations in perspective scale, there is not a great deal of insight that can be obtained from the currency values alone.

The currency values for Total Revenue for the organisations in this example were converted into AR values and depicted in Figure 6.18. The Total Revenue AR values of the benchmarked organisations in Figure 6.18 indicate that the revenue for SEW appears to be on par with the revenue for MW and SW. This figure also shows that, although the currency values for its revenue is much higher than that for MW, the revenue for SW is very similar to MW once it has been converted into AR values. Furthermore, despite being the smallest of the Australian organisations in terms of currency values for revenue, YVW was actually performing at a comparatively higher level than

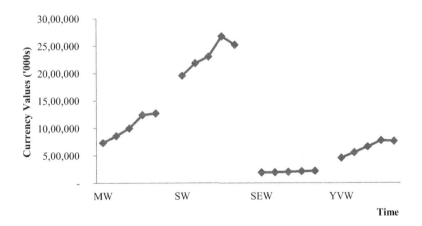

Figure 6.17 Currency values for total revenue for water agencies for 2009–2013.

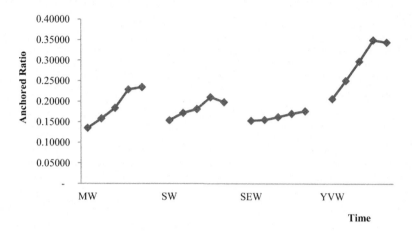

Figure 6.18 AR values for total revenue for water agencies for 2009–2013.

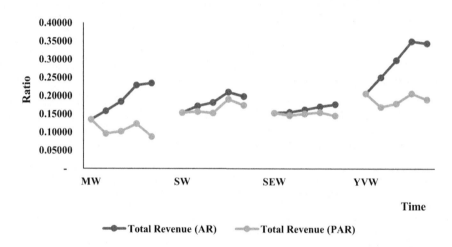

Figure 6.19 IRAM values for total revenue for water agencies for 2009–2013.

the other three entities. This makes intuitive sense once it is considered that, as a water retailer rather than a supplier, YVW will be selling the water at a higher price than it is purchasing it for (from MW). This relationship is even more supportable by the fact that the pattern of its revenue growth over the time frame of analysis is almost identical to that of MW.

The next step of the analysis involves overlaying the PAR values for Total Revenue over the AR values for the organisations in the example to complete the IRAM process. The results are depicted in Figure 6.19. It is clear from these results that the growth of Total Revenue over the time frame of the analysis for SW and SEW was relatively organic. This conclusion is derived from the fact that the disparity between the AR and PAR values for those organisations in Figure 6.19 was much less than that for MW and YVW.

It is understood, from the discussion in the previous section, that the results for MW were affected by two major shocks to the operations of the entity. It is intriguing that the results for YVW were almost identical in nature to those of MW. Not only was there a similar dramatic deviation between the two methods in 2010, but YVW also endured a similar additional negative deviation between the techniques in 2013. An analysis of the annual reports of YVW for those periods indicated that they similarly revalued their asset holdings in 2010 and were also affected by the desalination plant in 2013 (via a desalination plant rebate).

One of the advantages of the IRAM for non-profit or government bodies is that it is a system that does not rely on revenue or surpluses to assess the financial performance of an organisation. Given that expenditure items to fulfil programmes are the focus of most of these types of organisations, the IRAM is an excellent way to benchmark and compare the performance of such bodies in terms of their expenditure categories. The first category to demonstrate this utility is the Operational Expenses category for the entities in this example. The application of the IRAM to this category is illustrated in Figure 6.20. Of the four organisations depicted in Figure 6.20, MW clearly has the lowest level of expenditure for this category. This could (in a more commercial environment) signal a competitive advantage for MW. On the other end of the scale, YVW clearly has significantly higher Operational Expenses compared to its benchmarked entities. This could be a reflection of the fact that YVW is a retail body. Interestingly, although the numerical values of this category for YVW appears to be increasing significantly, the PAR values indicate a proportionately steady level of expenditure.

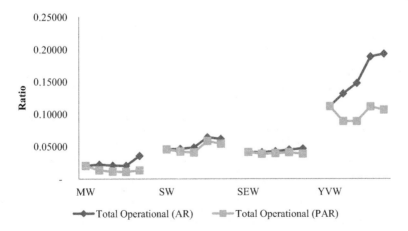

Figure 6.20 IRAM values for operational expenses for water agencies for 2009–2013.

The next expenditure category to be assessed is the Employee Benefits category. The application of the IRAM to this category is illustrated by Figure 6.21. Overall, the Employee Benefits for SW were much higher than any of the organisations in the benchmarked cohort. This suggests that the cost of labour for SW is higher than that for its Australian counterparts. The management of SW may benefit from reviewing the operations of those bodies in an effort to understand this category better with a view to identify any inefficiencies that could be eliminated to reduce the difference to the other bodies to a more similar level.

The final category for the application of the IRAM in this example is the Financial Expenses class. Depicted in Figure 6.22, the comparison for this

Figure 6.21 IRAM values for employee benefits for water agencies for 2009–2013.

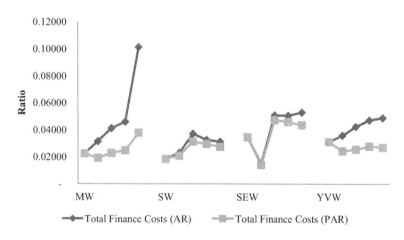

Figure 6.22 IRAM values for total finance costs for water agencies for 2009–2013.

category indicates that, apart from the additional finance expenses from the Desalination Plant in 2013, the expenditure in this category for MW was at similar levels to its benchmarked entities. If these organisations were commercial enterprises, the continued influence of this expense on the operations of MW in future would result in a sustained competitive disadvantage that others could have utilised to their advantage and may have resulted in the financial failure of this operation.

Case study: application of the IRAM to GM

Along with the Total Revenue and Total Costs and Expenses variables, the Operating Income /(loss) variable was selected for GM for the period 2009–2011 to demonstrate the IRAM. The AR and PAR values for these variables are depicted in Figure 6.23. It is clear, from the application of the IRAM to the trading statement variables for GM, that the very close similarity between the AR and PAR values for the Operating Income / (loss) variable was replicated for the variables that determine this value. It is, consequently, obvious that the growth of the financial variables for GM over the period of analysis was predominantly organic.

Assessment of the integrated ratio analysis methodology (IRAM)

It was shown in Chapter 5 that the AR technique produces ratios that faithfully reproduce the patterns of growth of their currency equivalents over time. It was shown in Chapter 4 that the PAR methodology produces ratios that indicate the specific proportionality for one period only. The benefit of combining the two methods into an integrated solution overcomes any

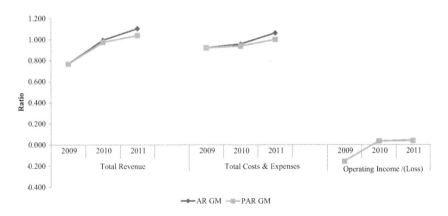

Figure 6.23 IRAM values for main trading statement categories for GM.

perceived limitations for either of its constituent parts. The AR values help to identify the growth of variables over time with an inherent context and instant comparability. The PAR values will illustrate whether that growth was a result of changes in the perspective scale of the operations of the business, or that the growth was actually a consequence of changes to the efficiency and effectiveness of the business.

In a similar vein to the statement made in the review of the AR technique, it may be that shortcomings of this integrated technique and the system overall may be discovered over time as its use becomes more widespread. Again, despite this possibility, the superior levels of reliability and comparability that this system provides in comparison to other available techniques should provide users of the system with an immense level of improved insight and utility. Indeed, because the system overcomes the issues that render other techniques fundamentally flawed, the IRAM should be considered the best process for financial performance measurement, assessment and benchmarking for any type of organisation.

Summary

Having developed the PAR technique in Chapter 4 and the AR technique in Chapter 5, this chapter demonstrated how the simultaneous application of the two approaches over time represented the complete IRAM advocated for in this book. The combined use of the AR and PAR techniques that form the IRAM as a system ensures that the advantages of each technique are maximised and any negative issues minimised. After describing how the complete methodology would work in practice, this chapter provided some important examples of how the system could help to generate significant business and competitive intelligence to assist management to better manage their organisations.

The adoption and implementation of the IRAM would be very simple for organisations to achieve. The direct benefits of more focused decision-making by managers from this objective would be improved financial performance and more sustainable operations. If an organisation is in a market that is open to economic competition (e.g. not a government agency), and the financial statements of that entity are publicly available, it would be possible for the competitors to conduct competitive intelligence of their own using the IRAM. This could reveal operational deficiencies and weaknesses that they could exploit and target in their strategic objectives. Therefore, it would be prudent that, at a minimum, your organisation is aware of what your financials could be revealing to your competitors if they use this system against your organisation.

References

ABC Learning, 2004. Annual Report 2004.
ABC Learning, 2005. Annual Report 2005.
ABC Learning, 2006. Annual Report 2006.

ABC Learning, 2007. Annual Report 2007.

GM, 2009. GM Annual Report 2009.

GM, 2010. GM Annual Report 2010.

GM, 2011. GM Annual Report 2011.

Melbourne Water, 2009. Melbourne Water, Annual Report 2009.

Melbourne Water, 2010. Melbourne Water, Annual Report 2010.

Melbourne Water, 2011. Melbourne Water, Annual Report 2011.

Melbourne Water, 2012. Melbourne Water, Annual Report 2012.

Melbourne Water, 2013. Melbourne Water, Annual Report 2013.

Melbourne Water 101, March 2020, https://www.melbournewater.com.au/about-us/who-we-are, pp. 1–32.

South East Water Limited, 2009. South East Water Limited, Annual Report 2009.

South East Water Limited, 2010. South East Water Limited, Annual Report 2010.

South East Water Limited, 2011. South East Water Limited, Annual Report 2011.

South East Water Limited, 2012. South East Water Limited, Annual Report 2012.

South East Water Limited, 2013. South East Water Limited, Annual Report 2013.

Sydney Water, 2009. Sydney Water, Annual Report 2009.

Sydney Water, 2010. Sydney Water, Annual Report 2010.

Sydney Water, 2011. Sydney Water, Annual Report 2011.

Sydney Water, 2012. Sydney Water, Annual Report 2012.

Sydney Water, 2013. Sydney Water, Annual Report 2013.

Yarra Valley Water, 2009. Yarra Valley Water, Annual Report 2009.

Yarra Valley Water, 2010. Yarra Valley Water, Annual Report 2010.

Yarra Valley Water, 2011. Yarra Valley Water, Annual Report 2011.

Yarra Valley Water, 2012. Yarra Valley Water, Annual Report 2012.

Yarra Valley Water, 2013. Yarra Valley Water, Annual Report 2013.

7 Summary and conclusion

Abstract

The need for a financial performance measurement scale that is able to validly convey both the quantum and quality of the performance was demonstrated in Chapter 1. This chapter also identified the issues that not only rendered currency inadequate for purpose, but also affected the most commonly utilised techniques intended to overcome these shortcomings. These issues included inconstant translation rates, lack of inherent context, temporal consistency, internal and external consistency, significance and perspective scale. The manner in which these identified issues affected currency as a measurement unit was explored in Chapter 2. This chapter utilised a number of examples and case studies to demonstrate how these issues resulted in currency being inadequate for purpose. This was, in turn, followed by an analysis of how these same issues also affected common techniques that were developed in an attempt to compensate for the shortcomings of currency. Chapter 3, therefore, examined how techniques such as percentage change, ratios, and horizontal and vertical analyses have been used in an attempt to measure and convey the financial performance of organisations. This chapter also demonstrated how these techniques were, ultimately, also inadequate.

In addition to identifying the deficiencies of current techniques, this book has proposed a methodology and system as a complete solution that overcomes these issues and satisfies the abilities required of a financial performance measurement scale. The solution consists of an algorithm that converts information contained in financial statements into normalised values. This algorithm is applied in two different time frames. The first application of the algorithm is to all of the data contained in the financial statements for one period. This version has been titled proportional asset ratio (PAR) analysis and was proposed and demonstrated in Chapter 4. The use of examples and case studies were employed in order to illustrate the advantages of this technique over current approaches. The second application of this algorithm involves applying the technique to information for multiple periods of time. This version has been titled the anchored ratio (AR) and was proposed and demonstrated in Chapter 5. The simultaneous and combined use of these two versions of the algorithm forms the integrated ratio analysis method (IRAM) proposed by this book. Suggested and demonstrated in Chapter 6, this system provides a means by which an analyst can determine the normalised values of the financial information in terms of their identical rates of growth to their currency values (the AR technique) in direct comparison to their organic growth (the PAR technique).

Introduction

The need for a financial performance measurement system is unquestioned. Unfortunately, the natural unit in which financial transactions are reported in (currency) does not possess the innate characteristics of a quality measurement scale. While there have been efforts to suggest alternatives to currency as a means of measuring financial performance, these efforts have tended to focus on improving the perceived utility of such systems rather than addressing the underlying causes of the shortcomings of currency as a measurement scale. This book has sought to address the apparent vacuum on this aspect in the literature by identifying how currency (and other popular techniques) does not possess the characteristics that a quality measurement unit should enjoy. Furthermore, this book has proposed a methodology that was shown to overcome the identified shortcomings of currency (and other popular techniques) as a financial performance measurement scale.

Summary

The need for a financial performance measurement scale that is able to validly convey both the quantum and quality of the performance was demonstrated in Chapter 1. This chapter also identified the issues that not only rendered currency inadequate for purpose, but also affected the most commonly utilised techniques intended to overcome these shortcomings. These issues included inconstant translation rates, lack of inherent context, temporal consistency, internal and external consistency, significance and perspective scale. The manner in which these identified issues affected currency as a measurement unit was explored in Chapter 2. This chapter utilised a number of examples and case studies to demonstrate how these issues resulted in currency being inadequate for purpose. This was, in turn, followed by an analysis of how these same issues also affected common techniques that were developed in an attempt to compensate for the shortcomings of currency. Chapter 3, therefore, examined how techniques such as percentage change, ratios, and horizontal and vertical analyses have been used in an attempt to measure and convey the financial performance of organisations. This chapter also demonstrated how these techniques were, ultimately, also inadequate.

In addition to identifying the deficiencies of current techniques, this book has proposed a methodology and system as a complete solution that overcomes these issues and satisfies the abilities required of a financial performance measurement scale. The solution consists of an algorithm that converts information contained in financial statements into normalised values. This algorithm is applied in two different time frames. The first application of the algorithm is to all of the data contained in the financial statements for one period. This version has been titled proportional asset ratio (PAR) analysis and was proposed and demonstrated in Chapter 4. The use of examples and case studies were employed in order to illustrate the advantages of this technique over current approaches. The second application of this algorithm involves applying the technique to information for multiple periods of time. This version has been titled the anchored ratio (AR) and was proposed and demonstrated in Chapter 5. The simultaneous and combined use of these two versions of the algorithm forms the integrated ratio analysis method (IRAM) proposed by this book. Suggested and demonstrated in Chapter 6, this system provides a means by which an analyst can determine the normalised values of the financial information in terms of their identical rates of growth to their currency values (the AR technique) in direct comparison to their organic growth (the PAR technique).

Conclusion

The financial performance of an organisation is a vital aspect of ensuring the longevity of that organisation. Consequently, the ability to properly measure and assess the quality of that performance ensures that the quality of that performance from an internal perspective, in comparison to other organisations, is a necessary requirement. This book has demonstrated that the system that has been promoted as a panacea to the issues that limit traditional approaches is able to overcome the shortcomings of those methods and also achieve the objectives for which it was developed. There are many uses for which the IRAM could be applied that depend upon the needs of the consumers of the information contained in the financial statements of organisations. Now that you are armed with an understanding of how the IRAM overcomes the issues identified and have been provided with examples of how it is to be applied and interpreted, this should ensure that you will maximise the utility that this technique offers you for whatever your needs are.

Index

Note: **Bold** page numbers refer to tables and *italic* page numbers refer to figures.

Printed in Great Britain
by Amazon

38920844R00086